The Optimum Growth Rate for Population in the Neoclassical Overlapping Generations Model

European University Studies
Europäische Hochschulschriften
Publications Universitaires Européennes

Series V
Economics and Management

Reihe V Série V
Volks- und Betriebswirtschaft
Sciences économiques, gestion d'entreprise

Vol./Bd. 3282

PETER LANG
Frankfurt am Main · Berlin · Bern · Bruxelles · New York · Oxford · Wien

Wolfgang Kuhle

The Optimum Growth Rate for Population in the Neoclassical Overlapping Generations Model

PETER LANG
Internationaler Verlag der Wissenschaften

Bibliographic Information published by the Deutsche Nationalbibliothek
The Deutsche Nationalbibliothek lists this publication in the Deutsche Nationalbibliografie; detailed bibliographic data is available in the internet at <http://www.d-nb.de>.

ISSN 0531-7339
ISBN 978-3-631-57352-5

www.peterlang.de

TO

MY PARENTS

Foreword

According to current projections, the population in the OECD countries is destined to shrink in the coming decades. In this context the problem of optimal population, with its long tradition in social science, is of renewed interest. This study inquires into the long-run implications of demographic change with respect to factor prices and individual welfare.

The Diamond (1965) model, which is a blend of the pure consumption loan economy of Samuelson (1958) and the neoclassical one-sector growth model, provides the natural framework for such an analysis. The study comprises a self contained exposition of the problem of optimal population in these three models. The ongoing discussion between Phelps (1966), Samuelson (1975), Jaeger (1989) and Michel and Pestieau (1993) on the existence of an interior optimum growth rate for population serves as the principal motivation for the main part of this inquiry.

The author derives exact general necessary and sufficient conditions for the existence of an interior optimum growth rate for an economy with and without pay-as-you-go financed social security/government debt. These conditions indicate that the individual will benefit from reductions in the growth rate for population as long as the economy is not experiencing dynamic inefficiency. For an economy with government debt, there is an ambiguous effect: the reduction in the growth rate for population leads to more favorable factor prices, but it reduces the internal rate of return of the pension scheme. Under these conditions it turns out that the Serendipity Theorem of Samuelson (1975) does not hold and that the growth rate for population, which leads the laissez faire economy to golden rule growth, can no longer be optimal. The formal discussion is complemented by verbal, empiric and diagrammatic illustrations.

Berlin, spring 2007 Klaus Jaeger

Foreword of the Author

This study is a revised version of my Diplom-Thesis, which was written at the Free University of Berlin in 2006. I am grateful to the second referee Professor Collier Ph.D. for introducing me to the neoclassical overlapping generations model. I was also supported by Nataliya Demchenko, Anneliese Kuhle and Juliane Jörgens.
In particular I have to thank my teacher Professor Dr. Klaus Jaeger, who brought the topic of this thesis to my attention and who was always available for an open discussion.

Mannheim, spring 2007 Wolfgang Kuhle

Contents

List of Figures

List of Tables

1. Introduction

The objective of this Inquiry is to summarize and supplement the discussion on the optimum growth rate for population in the neoclassical overlapping generations model. In order to allow for a self-contained treatment the focus will be on the most fundamental aspects of this discussion: the interrelation between the growth rate of population, the intertemporal and intergenerational consumption patterns, and the accumulation of capital.

Among all simplifying assumptions which have to be made, the most severe simplification is that the growth rate of population will be treated as an exogenous variable, which can be set to different levels by an imaginary authority. Even under these benign conditions the results from the formal analysis will remain to a certain extent ambiguous.

The problem of optimal population in the neoclassical overlapping generations model is "non-convex"[1] and hence it is not treated in the common textbooks on neoclassical growth theory. The key references which explicitly treat the problem of optimum population are: Samuelson (1958), Phelps (1967a), Samuelson (1975a), Deardorff (1976), Samuelson (1976), Arthur and McNicoll (1978), Jaeger (1989), Michel and Pestieau (1993) and Jaeger (2002). The basic elements of the neoclassical overlapping generations model are taken from the essays of Solow (1956), Samuelson (1958), Phelps (1961), Samuelson (1962), Diamond (1965), Cass and Yaari (1966) and the textbooks of Blanchard and Fischer (1989) and De La Croix and Michel (2002). At certain points, where the theoretical results are ambiguous, we will also refer to recent empiric

[1] De La Croix and Michel (2002), (p. 172).

evidence provided by de Abreu Pessoa et al. (2005), Guvenen (2002), Ogaki and Reinhart (1998) and our own, to evaluate the significance of these theoretical findings.

1.1. Historical Perspective

The discussion on the subject of optimal population can be traced back to ancient times and hence it seems interesting to give a very brief outline of a few different perspectives which have evolved over time:

1. In ancient Greece one can find a clear emphasis on an optimal plateau for population: Plato suggests that the optimal size for a Polis is 5040 (7!) citizens. Hippodamos suggests an optimal number of 10.000 citizens. Aristotle, who considered these numbers as being too large, saw overpopulation as one of the main causes of unrest, instability and poverty. The only exception in ancient Greece was Sparta which suffered from a continuous decline in the number of Spartiats. For the Roman republic as well as the Roman empire one can find that high fertility rates were always encouraged.[2]

2. The stance taken by Malthus (1992)[3] is that humankind would procreate to the point where, due to finite natural resources, the standard of living falls to the level of mere subsistence.

3. A different perspective is advocated by Meade (1937), (pp. 255-284): In an economy with finite natural resources, where initially

[2]Wilkinson (1978), (pp. 443-444).
[3]First published in 1798.

there exist scale economies which originate from a better division of labor, there is an optimal finite size for population and the aggregate capital stock. Optimal in the sense that per capita real income is maximized.

4. Keynes (1978), (pp. 518-519)[4] and others argue that a growing population allows for a better division of labor, lower unemployment due to a higher flexibility of the workforce, and a larger military potential, i.e. a more benign environment for economic activity. Another advantage, according to this view, is that aggregate demand will increase faster and that misjudgments on the side of investors, which lead to a temporary oversupply of certain capital goods, are corrected more quickly. The accelerator principle and greater optimism will add to these positive effects.[5]

5. In the framework of the conventional neoclassical growth model – where an aggregate constant returns to scale production function describes the relation between output and the two input factors capital and labor – the size of population becomes irrelevant. Due to the assumption of constant returns to scale, which implies that natural resources are abundant or that land-augmenting technical progress takes place at a sufficiently high rate, it is now the growth rate for population which is decisive for per capita income. Contrary to the historically predominant stances with their emphasis on a plateau for population, the emphasis is now on an optimum growth path for population.

[4]First published in 1937.

[5]Jaeger (1972), (pp. 11-14).

1.2. Main Assumptions and Method of Analysis

Throughout this inquiry, comparative dynamic[6] analysis is employed, i.e. only steady state equilibria are considered. This means that the focus is solely on the long-run implications of changes in the exogenously given growth rate of population. The effects during the period of transition from one stable population to another, which might exceed the lifetime of an individual, will be put aside.

In general two scenarios will be considered: a) a planning framework where an imaginary central authority can set all quantities to their respective optimal levels, and b) a laissez faire framework where the imaginary authority can only vary the growth rate of population. Compared to our main references we will put a stronger emphasis on the discussion of the laissez faire economy and develop a detailed diagrammatic exposition.

In the overlapping generations framework we will follow Blanchard and Fischer (1989) and assume the existence of a stable and unique steady state equilibrium. The stability conditions will then be used to evaluate the comparative dynamic behavior of the economy as in Samuelson (1941) and Diamond (1965).

The main assumptions with respect to the production function, the distribution of income, and the ordinal utility function of the representative individual will be introduced as we proceed.

The criterion for optimal population: The growth rate of population which maximizes steady state utility of the representative indi-

[6] Jaeger (1980), (p. 80).

vidual will be considered as being "optimal". There will be some exceptions where this utility criterion is inapplicable; in such cases per capita consumption or the economic dependency ratio will serve as alternative *individualistic* criteria. The Benthamite "total utility criterion", which in general leads to higher optimum growth rates for population, will not be applied.[7]

Organization: The following three chapters contain:

1. Our theoretical starting point in Chapter 2 will be the consumption-loan model of Samuelson (1958) and the one-sector neoclassical growth model of Solow (1956). These two models allow to isolate the crucial components to the problem of optimal population. In a next step, the Diamond (1965) model without government debt will be used to derive the two-part golden rule and the necessary and sufficient conditions for the optimum growth rate for population in a planned as well as in a laissez faire economy. Towards the end, the Serendipity Theorem will be derived and a diagrammatic summary will be given.

2. The intention in Chapter 3 is to reconsider the validity of the key results which were obtained in Chapter 2 under highly idealized conditions. Two aspects will be considered:

   (a) child-dependency costs;

   (b) government debt.

[7] A proof that the total utility criterion leads to higher optimum growth rates than the individualistic average utility criterion is given in Nerlove et al. (1986), (pp. 7-8).

3. Chapter 4 contains an alternative approach to the problem of optimal population, which is based on the economic dependency ratio. This approach is related to the problem of child-dependency costs in Chapter 3.

2. The Optimum Growth Rate for Population in the Neoclassical Growth Model

The purpose of this chapter is to summarize the main elements of the discussion concerning the optimal growth rate for population in the neoclassical framework. The core of the subject is going to be the interrelation between the growth rate of population, the intertemporal and intergenerational consumption patterns, and the accumulation of capital. In order to concentrate on these elements, further aspects like technical progress, endogenous fertility, child-dependency costs, external effects, altruism and scarce natural resources will be left out of consideration.

The question will be approached by singling out the advantages and disadvantages of high (low) growth rates of population. In order to isolate the advantages of high population growth rates, a consumption-loan model following Samuelson (1958) will be used. The disadvantages of high growth rates of population can be isolated in the framework of the Solow (1956) growth model.

In a second step, the Diamond (1965) model will be briefly introduced. In contrast to the Solow growth model and the consumption-loan model, the Diamond model allows to weigh between advantages and disadvantages of an increase or a decrease in the growth rate of population. In the framework of the Diamond model, both of the effects which were isolated before reappear, and, depending on the specifications of the model, an optimal intermediate rate of population growth may exist. In this part the main references will be Phelps (1967a), Samuelson (1968), Samuelson (1975a), Samuelson (1976), Deardorff (1976) and Michel and

Pestieau (1993).

In the last part we leave the discussion of the planned optimum and turn towards the discussion of the optimum growth rate for population in a laissez faire economy.

2.1. The Optimum Growth Rate for Population in the Consumption-Loan Model

2.1.1. The Model

The consumption-loan model falls into the category of overlapping generation models introduced by Allais (1947), Samuelson (1958), and Diamond (1965). The name is related to its structure: at any given time t there are always two or more generations alive and these generations may or may not engage in trade with each other.

Since the sole purpose of this section is to identify the advantages of high growth rates of population, a two-period model will be used instead of the more complex three-period model. People live for two periods. In the first period of their lifetime each individual earns one unit of an exogenously given output. In the second period of life each individual lives in retirement.

At time t there are N_t young people and N_{t-1} old people alive, the subscript is indicating the date of birth. Furthermore, nobody dies after the first period of life. The population grows at an exogenously given rate of n such that:

$$N_{t+1} = (1+n)N_t. \tag{1}$$

Production: As mentioned above, each young individual earns one unit of exogenously given output. Thus, output for the whole economy at time t is N_t. No capital or scarce land is being used in the production process and output is assumed to be nondurable.

The Utility Function: Each individual derives utility from the consumption at the end of the first and second period of life. The ordinal utility function is given by: [8]

$$U = U(c^1, c^2). \tag{2}$$

This utility function is assumed to have the following properties:

$$U_{c^1}(c^1, c^2) > 0; \qquad U_{c^2}(c^1, c^2) > 0,$$

$$\begin{aligned} \lim_{c_1 \to \infty} U_{c^1}(c^1, c^2) &= 0; & \lim_{c_2 \to \infty} U_{c^2}(c^1, c^2) &= 0, \\ \lim_{c_1 \to 0} U_{c^1}(c^1, c^2) &= \infty; & \lim_{c_2 \to 0} U_{c^2}(c^1, c^2) &= \infty, \end{aligned}$$

$$U_{c^1c^1} < 0; \quad U_{c^2c^2} < 0; \quad U_{c^1c^2} = U_{c^2c^1} \gtrless 0,$$

$$U_{c^1c^1}U_{c^2c^2} - U_{c^1c^2}^2 > 0.$$

The assumptions made in the last two rows ensure that the utility function is strictly concave.

2.1.2. The Social Optimum

In the following we will search for the optimal consumption pattern c^{1*}, c^{2*} and the optimal growth rate of population n^*. Optimal in the sense

[8] Concerning the notation: $U_{c^i} := \frac{\partial U}{\partial c^i}$; $\qquad U_{c^ic^j} := \frac{\partial^2 U}{\partial c^i \partial c^j}$.

that the steady state utility of the representative individual is maximized. It will be assumed that the social planner can set the growth rate of population to any desired level. According to the assumptions made on production and output, there is the following budget or "availability" constraint (Samuelson (1958), p. 473):

$$N_t c_t^1 + N_{t-1} c_t^2 = 1 \cdot N_t \Leftrightarrow c_t^1 + \frac{c_t^2}{1+n} = 1. \tag{3}$$

Equation (3) states that for each period the aggregate consumption of the old and young individuals equals aggregate output. Thus the social planner faces the following maximization problem:[9]

$$\max_{n,c^1,c^2} U(c^1, c^2) \qquad \text{s.t.} \quad c^1 + \frac{c^2}{1+n} = 1; \qquad c^1, c^2 > 0.$$

Using the Lagrange method we have:

$$\max_{c^1,c^2,n,\lambda} \quad \mathcal{L}(c^1, c^2, n, \lambda) = U(c^1, c^2) + \lambda(1 - c^1 - \frac{c^2}{1+n}). \tag{4}$$

With the first order conditions:

$$\frac{\partial \mathcal{L}}{\partial c^1} = U_{c^1} - \lambda = 0, \tag{5}$$

$$\frac{\partial \mathcal{L}}{\partial c^2} = U_{c^2} - \frac{\lambda}{(1+n)} = 0, \tag{6}$$

$$\frac{\partial \mathcal{L}}{\partial n} = \frac{\lambda c^2}{(1+n)^2} = 0, \tag{7}$$

$$\frac{\partial \mathcal{L}}{\partial \lambda} = 1 - c^1 - \frac{c^2}{(1+n)} = 0. \tag{8}$$

[9] Which generally corresponds to the problem solved by Samuelson (1958), but differs with respect to n, which is an additional choice variable. As in Samuelson (1958) the time index is omitted because only steady states are considered.

These four conditions implicitly define the optimal values λ^*, c^{1*}, c^{2*} and n^*. The conditions (5) and (6) combined give the "biological interest rate relation" of Samuelson (1958):

$$\frac{U_{c^1}}{U_{c^2}} = (1+n). \tag{9}$$

Condition (9) describes how the available resources at each point in time should be allocated among the young generation and the current old generation. This is illustrated in Diagram 1. Condition (8) is a restatement of the budget constraint and (7) is the condition for the optimal n^*. A closer look at (7) reveals that this condition cannot be satisfied. From (5) we know that λ^*, which is the marginal utility of income, must be positive. Since λ^*, c^{2*} and $(1+n^*)^2$ are all positive, $\frac{\partial \mathcal{L}}{\partial n}$ must be positive too. This means that every increase in n increases the value of the objective function. The larger n the less binding is the budget constraint and the higher is the utility of the representative individual. Every increase in n makes future consumption cheaper. People in their old age are supported by a larger group of young people who receive the exogenously given income. The age distribution of the population is permanently skewed in favor of the productive ages (Samuelson (1958), p. 472). If there was a maximum feasible growth rate n^{max}, the social planner would choose $n^* = n^{max}$.[10]

[10]Such an additional restriction could be accounted for by introducing a term $\mu(n - n^{max})$ into our Lagrange function. The resulting FOC would now be of the Kuhn-Tucker type.

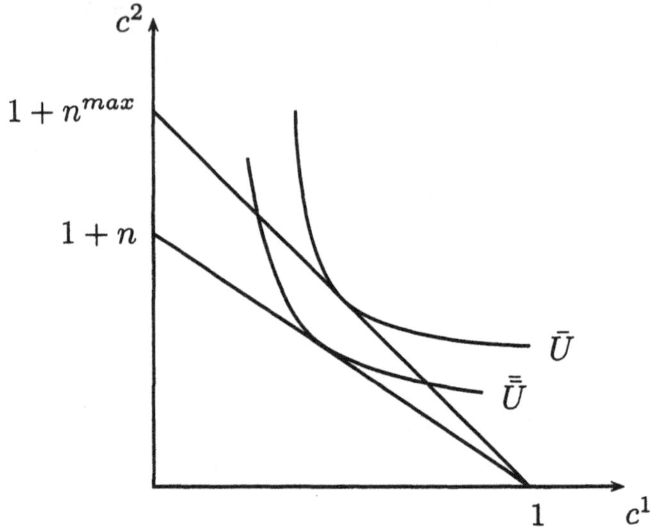

Diagram 1: *The biological interest rate relation and utility.*

2.1.3. The Individual Utility Maximization

From the perspective of the representative individual, the problem is to maximize utility by choosing the optimal values of consumption for a given interest rate r and a given income of one unit. It consumes c^1 in the first period of life and gives a loan of $(1-c^1)$ to somebody else.[11] In the second period it consumes principal and interest, which amounts to $(1-c^1)(1+r)$. Hence the representative individual behaves as follows:

$$\max_{c^1,c^2} U(c^1,c^2) \qquad \text{s.t.} \quad c^1 + \frac{c^2}{1+r} = 1; \qquad c^1, c^2 > 0. \tag{10}$$

[11]The problem that there is nobody in the market who demands loans will be discussed later.

Using the Lagrange method the following first order necessary conditions are obtained:

$$U_{c^1} = \lambda, \quad (11)$$

$$\frac{U_{c^1}}{U_{c^2}} = (1+r), \quad (12)$$

$$c^1 + \frac{c^2}{1+r} = 1. \quad (13)$$

These three equations implicitly define the optimal values $\tilde{c^1}$, $\tilde{c^2}$ and $\tilde{\lambda}$ for the representative individual. If the market interest rate r happens to be equal to n^*, conditions (11)-(13) would implicitly define the same optimal values c^{1*}, c^{2*}, λ^* which were previously found by the social planner from conditions (5), (6) and (8). If r does not happen to be equal to n^*, the social optimum will not be attained. The values $\tilde{c^1}$, $\tilde{c^2}$ and $\tilde{\lambda}$ will differ from the optimal values c^{1*}, c^{2*}, λ^*.

As Samuelson (1958) points out, the market interest rate r will not automatically, i.e. by competition, evolve into the desired biological rate of interest where r equals n. Instead r will fall short of the biological rate of interest n. In our case with only two overlapping generations the interest rate will be at $r = -1$ and trade between the generations would be impossible. This stems from the special two generations case.

Only young people would be willing to supply loans, but nobody can ever take a loan and repay it afterwards.[12] Thus there is a lack of borrowing in the loan market. Hence the social planner has to find a measure to

[12]The young individual tries to spread its exogenous income over its two period life-cycle. Hence the young individual would like to give a loan to somebody. The only ones who would like to borrow are the (needy) current old. However since the old generation has no income, and the old generation will not be around in the next period, they can never repay any loans.

force $r = n$. Otherwise the favorable effects of high population growth rates do not come into play, since every individual would choose $\tilde{c}^1 = 1$ and $\tilde{c}^2 = 0$. This result is fundamentally altered in the three generations case, which allows for different market transactions. This case is treated by Samuelson (1958), but, since we do not have the space to cover this discussion concerning dynamic inefficiency without externalities, we will stop here and allow for financial intermediation by the government.

2.1.4. Financial Intermediation by the Government

In order to enforce the benefits of high population growth rates, the government has to ensure that the market interest rate r equals n. As Samuelson (1958), Samuelson (1959), Lerner (1959) and Cass and Yaari (1966) discuss, the problem of a lack of borrowing in the market can be solved via two ways: one is to introduce money as a store of value, the other is to open a government-owned loan-bank. If money was introduced into the system, young individuals could buy money and carry it over into the period of retirement in order to sell it to the next young generation. The central bank which issues the money would take the role of a debtor in the economy (Cass and Yaari (1966), p. 362).

Since Cass et al. (1979) showed that money in a consumption-loan model is a complicated matter, we will introduce a government-owned consumption-loan bank as discussed in Cass and Yaari (1966), (pp. 359-362).

This bank offers each young individual an interest rate of $n^*(> r = -1)$. Every young individual will now voluntarily deposit savings that amount to $(1-c^{1*})$ in this bank, in order to receive $c^{2*} = (1+n^*)(1-c^{1*})$

in the retirement period. As mentioned above, the reason for this is that once there is a higher market interest rate of n^*, the individual utility maximization problem becomes the same as the one solved by the social planner. The first order conditions of the individual (11)-(13) are equal to the conditions (5), (6), and (8), which describe the social optimum.

The government-owned loan-bank works as follows: at time t the bank takes new loans amounting to $N_t(1 - c^{1*})$ and pays back old loans amounting to $N_{t-1}c^{2*}$. This is obviously a chain letter situation. The bank is loosing money on every contract, but it can always exactly repay the old debt by starting a new contract which is $(1+n)$ times bigger than the old one.[13] The retired generation at the time when the "bank" is started are winners in any case, because they receive $c^{2*} = (1+n^*)(1-c^{1*})$ without having saved in the first period of life. If the time horizon is infinite, this is not a problem, because there are always new generations coming along and the accumulated debt will be passed on forever. With an infinite horizon everybody will be better off if a government-run loan-bank is established. If the time horizon is finite, however, the last generation will be worse off, because they will have to repay the accumulated debt.

2.1.5. Provisional Result

In the foregoing section, the advantages of high population growth rates in the very artificial case of the consumption-loan model with an exogenous per capita income were examined. It turned out that a social

[13]The new loan is sufficient to exactly repay the old debt because: $N_t(1 - c^{1*}) = N_{t-1}c^{2*} = N_{t-1}(1 + n^*)(1 - c^{1*})$.

planner would set the growth rate of population n to the highest feasible level. In a second step it was found that individual utility maximization will not automatically lead to the desired social optimum. In the two-period case any trade between the generations is impossible. There is a lack of borrowing in the market. This problem can be solved by setting up a government-owned (chain letter) consumption-loan bank, which offers the biological rate of interest n^*.

2.2. The Optimum Growth Rate for Population in the Neoclassical One-sector Growth Model

In contrast to the consumption-loan model of Samuelson (1958), the neoclassical one-sector growth model is built around the production function, and capital formation plays a pivotal role. By following Solow (1956), Phelps (1961), Phelps (1967a) and Jones (1975), the negative effects of high population growth rates will be identified.

Using the fundamental equation of neoclassical growth, the first golden rule of capital accumulation for a given growth rate n will be derived. The main result in this section will be that high growth rates of population have a negative impact on per capita consumption and that this negative effect stems from the need to widen capital.

2.2.1. The Solow Growth Model

Population: In contrast to the population in the consumption-loan model, individuals live for an infinite time. Each individual supplies one unit of labor inelastically. Population grows according to:

$$N(t) = N_0 e^{nt}. \tag{14}$$

The growth rate of population n is exogenously given. The aggregate income of the households is used on consumption and savings:

$$Y = C + sY; \qquad 0 < s < 1. \tag{15}$$

The fraction of income saved s is exogenously given.

Production: The production function is assumed to be a substitutional, continuous, constant returns to scale, aggregate production function:

$$Y = F(K, N). \tag{16}$$

Using the assumption of constant returns to scale, equation (16) can be written in the intensive form:

$$y = f(k), \tag{17}$$

with

$$y := \frac{Y}{N}; \qquad k := \frac{K}{N}.$$

The production function is assumed to be strictly concave in k and to satisfy the Inada conditions:[14]

$$f'(k) > 0; \quad f''(k) < 0,$$

$$\lim_{k \to \infty} f'(k) = 0; \quad \lim_{k \to 0} f'(k) = \infty,$$

$$f(0) = 0; \quad f(\infty) = \infty.$$

[14]The Inada conditions are sufficient for the existence of a unique steady state equilibrium with a capital intensity (capital-labor ratio) of $k = \tilde{k} > 0$.

According to (15), the homogenous output produced can be either consumed or saved. The savings become automatically part of the society's total capital stock K. The aggregate savings go automatically into the formation of new capital and into the replacement of deprecated capital:[15]

$$sY = \dot{K} + \delta K. \tag{18}$$

The rate of deprecation δ is exogenously given.

Factor-prices and Income Distribution: According to the profit maximizing behavior of the private entrepreneur, the input factors capital and labor are payed their marginal product:[16]

$$r = F_K = \frac{\partial(Nf(k))}{\partial K} = f'(k), \tag{19}$$

$$w = F_N = \frac{\partial(Nf(k))}{\partial N} = f(k) - f'(k)k. \tag{20}$$

Using equations (19), (20) and the assumption of constant returns to scale, the Euler theorem can be derived:[17]

$$f(k) = w + rk \quad \Leftrightarrow \quad F(K, N) = F_N N + F_K K. \tag{21}$$

This theorem states that if factors are paid their marginal product, the whole income will be exhausted. The share of profits of the output is a function of the capital intensity:

[15]Savings automatically become capital because there is no distinction between individuals who save and individuals who make investments (Jones (1975), pp. 72-73).

[16]In the following r will be the gross real interest rate including deprecation. The net real interest rate is thus $r - \delta$.

[17]Proofs of the Euler theorem and the following statements in this paragraph are given, for example, in Chiang and Wainwright (2005).

$$\pi(k) := \frac{F_K K}{Y} = \frac{f'(k)k}{f(k)}. \tag{22}$$

The elasticity of substitution τ is also a function of the capital intensity:

$$\tau(k) := -\frac{(\frac{r}{w})}{k}\frac{dk}{d(\frac{r}{w})}. \tag{23}$$

Differentiation of (21) reveals that:[18]

$$F_{KN} = F_{NK} > 0. \tag{24}$$

After having introduced the production function and the Euler theorem, we can complete the picture of factor-prices and income distribution by introducing the factor-price frontier:[19]

$$w = \phi(r); \quad \frac{dw}{dr} = \phi'(r) = -k; \quad \frac{d^2w}{dr^2} = \phi''(r) = \frac{-1}{f''(k)}. \tag{25}$$

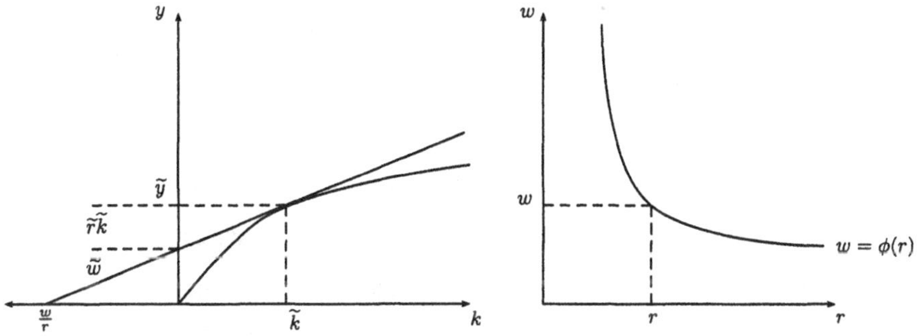

Diagram 2: *Factor-prices and income distribution.*

[18]According to Young's theorem, F_{KN} and F_{NK} are equal as long as we assume that they are both continuous.

[19]A discussion of the factor price frontier is given in Samuelson (1962), Jaeger (1980) or Jones (1975), (pp. 130-135). The properties in (25) are also derived in Appendix (B).

The Fundamental Equation of Neoclassical Growth: Under the assumptions made on the production function, output, savings, and population growth, by using (14), (15), (17), (18), and the growth rate of the capital intensity, the following can be obtained:

$$\frac{\dot{k}}{k} = \frac{\dot{K}}{K} - \frac{\dot{N}}{N} = \frac{sY - \delta K}{K} - n = \frac{N\left(\frac{sY}{N} - \delta(\frac{K}{N})\right)}{K} - n. \tag{26}$$

Multiplying (26) with k yields the fundamental equation of neoclassical growth:

$$\dot{k} = sf(k) - (n + \delta)k. \tag{27}$$

This first-order differential equation (27) implicitly describes the time path of the capital intensity. Since all other endogenous variables of the model depend on the capital intensity, equation (27) is referred to as the central equation of neoclassical growth. This central equation indicates that there are two crucial components which determine the path of the capital intensity: one is the exogenously given savings behavior, the other is the need to widen capital and to replace depreciated capital.

The Properties of Steady State Growth: A steady state growth path is defined as a path where all variables are growing at a constant proportional rate.[20] This does not mean that all variables must grow at the same proportional rate. The central equation indicates that such a path of growth is reached once the growth rate of the capital intensity $\frac{\dot{k}}{k}$ is zero. A constant capital intensity implies that the aggregate capital stock has to grow at the same constant exogenously given rate at which the population is growing. A constant k leaves factor-prices, per

[20] A classification of the different types of economic equilibria is given in Jaeger (1981), (pp. 675-677).

capita income, per capita consumption and savings unchanged; hence the aggregate output grows at the same constant rate as the population. Equation (27) also exhibits that $(n+\delta)$ must be positive to allow for such a steady state path. If only steady state paths are considered, this puts a technical restriction on the lowest feasible growth rate of population. However, since real world deprecation is much larger than the growth rate of population this is a rather theoretical problem.

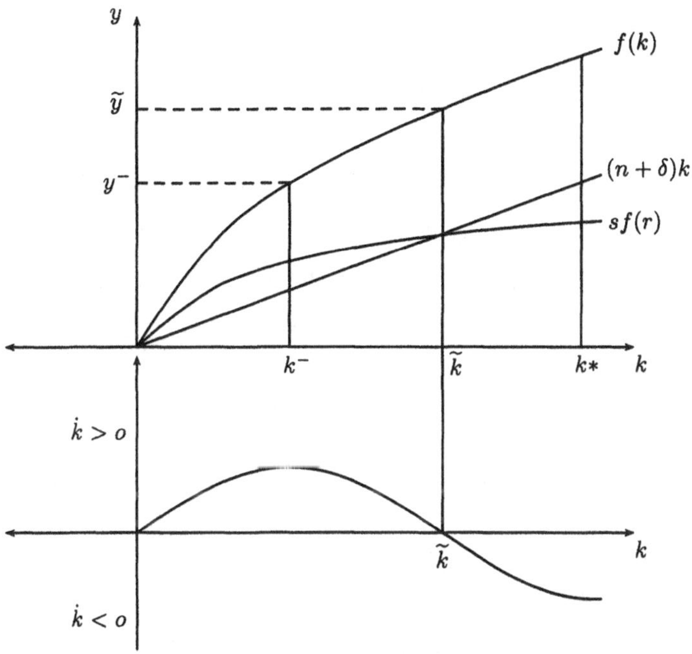

Diagram 3: *An illustration of the fundamental equation of neoclassical growth.*

Stability Condition: Taking the first derivative of $\dot{k}$ with respect to k, the stability conditions for the steady state equilibrium can be obtained:

$$\frac{d\dot{k}}{dk} = sf'(k) - (n + \delta) \lesseqgtr 0. \tag{28}$$

By using (27) and the assumption of a diminishing marginal productivity of capital, the sign of (28) around the equilibrium point at $\tilde{k}$ can be obtained. Since the marginal product of capital is always smaller than the average product of capital, we have:

$$\frac{d\dot{k}}{dk} = sf'(\tilde{k}) - (n + \delta) < 0. \tag{29}$$

This means that a rise (fall) in k above (below) $\tilde{k}$ leads to a declining (rising) k and the economy falls (grows) back to the old steady state equilibrium level. Equation (28) and Diagram 3 reconfirm that $(n + \delta)$ must be positive, otherwise the sign of $\frac{d\dot{k}}{dk}$ would be necessarily positive, which would make the system unstable.

2.2.2. The First Golden Rule of Capital Accumulation

The central equation (27) can now be used to derive the condition for optimal capital accumulation.[21]

In contrast to the consumption-loan model where an ordinal utility function was used as the welfare criterion, the Solow model does not contain such a utility function. Instead, per capita consumption will serve as the criterion.

[21] In the following we will refer to this first golden rule as the Phelps (1961) golden rule, even though it was discovered by numerous other economists at the same time.

Since all endogenous variables in the Solow model depend on the per capita capital stock, the social planner will have to choose k such that $c(k)$ is maximized. By using (15) and (27) the problem is:

$$\max_k c(k) = f(k) - (n + \delta)k. \tag{30}$$

This yields the first order necessary condition:

$$f'(k) - \delta = n. \tag{31}$$

First order condition (31) states that the net real interest rate $f'(k) - \delta$ must be equal to the growth rate of population n. The condition (31) implicitly defines an optimal $k^*(n, \delta)$.[22] In order to enforce the optimal steady state characterized by $k^*(n, \delta)$, the social planner can, using (27) with $\dot{k} = 0$, find the optimal savings ratio s^*:

$$s^* = \frac{f'(k^*)k^*}{f(k^*)}. \tag{32}$$

Characteristics of the Golden Rule path: The first order condition for the capital intensity states that in a golden rule steady state the net real interest rate on capital must equal the growth rate of population (Phelps (1961), p. 641). If the capital intensity is raised above k^*, the increment in output is not sufficient to offset the negative effect of additional capital widening, which is needed to keep the capital intensity constant. By using equations (27) and (31), the golden rule steady state can be characterized as a state where the share of income of capital equals the savings ratio and the investment ratio:

$$s^* = \frac{S}{F(K, L)} = \frac{I}{F(K, L)} = \pi(k^*). \tag{33}$$

[22]The second order condition for a maximum is also satisfied: $\frac{d^2c}{dk^2} = f''(k) < 0$.

Thus, if there is an economy where the long-run savings ratio and the investment ratio are equal to the share of capital income, this economy is in a long-run equilibrium with maximal per capita consumption (Phelps (1961), p. 641).

Along the lines of condition (31) there is another distinction which can be made concerning the dynamic efficiency: every economy with a capital intensity $k^H > k^*$ is in a dynamically inefficient state. Lowering the capital intensity increases current and future consumption.

Every economy with a capital intensity of $k^L < k^*$ is in an dynamically efficient state. The increased long-run (steady state) consumption comes at the cost of lower consumption during the period of transition. In the framework of the basic Solow model there is no criterion to decide whether the capital intensity should be increased or not.

2.2.3. The Disadvantages of High Rates of Population Growth

The influence of the population growth rate n on per capita consumption in the golden rule steady state can be found by taking the first derivative of per capita consumption with respect to the growth rate of population; utilizing (30) and $k^*(n, \delta)$ gives:

$$\frac{dc(k^*(n,\delta))}{dn} = \frac{d(f(k^*) - (n+\delta)k^*)}{dn} = f'(k^*)\frac{dk^*}{dn} - (n+\delta)\frac{dk^*}{dn} - k^*.$$

Recalling condition (31) one obtains:

$$\frac{dc(k^*(n,\delta))}{dn} = -k^* < 0. \tag{34}$$

Equation (34) indicates that each increase in the growth rate of population causes per capita consumption to fall (Phelps (1967a), p. 178). The reason for this result is that each individual which is born needs to be equipped with additional capital amounting to k^*. The resources needed for this kind of capital widening are foregone consumption to the rest of the population. Since capital widening, in contrast to capital deepening, does not increase per capita consumption, it can be considered as a waste of resources.

2.2.4. Provisional Result

This section was focused on the disadvantages of high growth rates of population. The analysis of the Solow (1956) model indicated that the population should grow at the lowest feasible rate. Due to the stability conditions and the first order condition (31) discussed above, this lowest feasible rate would be found at $n = -\delta$. According to the assumptions made on the production function, the best golden age with $n = -\delta$ would be characterized by an infinite capital intensity and infinite per capita output.

The negative effect of high population growth rates stems from the need for capital widening, which costs resources.

2.3. The Optimum Growth Rate of Population in the Diamond Neoclassical Growth Model

In the two preceding sections the results were clear: in a consumption-loan economy the representative individual benefits from high population growth by standing on the shoulders of many young and active workers; the social planner will set n to the highest feasible level. The opposite is true in the Solow model where high population growth leads to a waste of resources on capital widening and the lowest feasible n would be best.

In this section it will be analyzed how these two effects overlay each other. The Diamond (1965) model will be used to examine whether or not an optimal intermediate growth rate of population exists. The Diamond model is a blend of both: the Solow (1956) model and the overlapping generations model of Samuelson (1958). The population consists of two overlapping generations, which is important for the positive effects of population growth. On the other side, there is capital as an input-factor, which brings the negative effect of capital widening into play. A crucial difference between the Solow model and the Diamond model can be found in the savings function. In the Solow model the fraction of income saved was an exogenous constant; the Diamond model features an endogenously determined savings behavior. Individuals save in their young productive years to provide for their unproductive years of retirement and these savings lead to capital formation.

The idea of an optimum growth rate for population in the neoclassical overlapping generations model was first brought up by Phelps (1967a). However, the more clear and conclusive treatment was given by Samuelson (1975a).

The discussion of the optimum growth rate of population between Phelps (1967a), Samuelson (1968), Samuelson (1975a), Samuelson (1975b), Deardorff (1976), Samuelson (1976) and Michel and Pestieau (1993) is arranged as follows: In a first step we derive the necessary and sufficient conditions for a social optimum. The next part is dedicated to the laissez faire behavior of the economy and the Serendipity Theorem. The last part will contain further normative and positive aspects concerning the optimum growth rate of population in a laissez faire economy.

2.3.1. The Model

Population: The generations overlap in the same way as in the consumption-loan model. Population growth is again given by equation (1). There are no child-dependency costs and there is no altruism between the generations. Each individual is driven by its individual utility maximization problem. The individuals are assumed to hold the ordinal utility function (2).

Production: Production is described by the standard neoclassical production function given by (16). As in Diamond (1965), the young generation is supplying labor and the old generation is supplying the capital. The factors are paid according to their marginal productivity.

The Availability Constraint: Unlike the central equation (27) of the Solow model which was a first order differential equation, we will now face a first order difference equation. The need to treat time as a discrete variable stems from the structure of the overlapping generations model where individuals make their decisions concerning consumption and savings at certain points in time. The availability constraint for the social planner can be obtained by considering the use of total output in the economy on net investment, consumption and replacement of capital:

$$Y(K_t, N_t) = K_{t+1} - K_t + N_t c_t^1 + N_{t-1} c_t^2 + \delta K_t. \tag{35}$$

By dividing (35) through N_t we obtain:

$$k_{t+1} - k_t = f(k_t) - c_t^1 - \frac{c_t^2}{1+n} - nk_{t+1} - \delta k_t. \tag{36}$$

The steady state is again characterized by a constant capital labor ratio, that means:

$$k_{t+1} = k_t = k \quad \forall t. \tag{37}$$

Substituting (37) into (36) gives:

$$f(k) = c_t^1 + \frac{c_t^2}{1+n} + (n+\delta)k. \tag{38}$$

In what follows we will, again, consider steady states only, thus the time index can be omitted.

2.3.2. The Social Optimum

Instead of going through the analysis of the individual behavior and the laissez faire equilibrium, we will first follow Diamond (1965), Samuelson (1968) and Samuelson (1975a) in deriving the first order conditions for the social optimum.

The problem of the social planner is to maximize steady state lifetime utility of the representative individual, subject to the available per capita income in each period, by choosing the optimal quantities c^{1*}, c^{2*}, k^* and n^* (choosing n means also choosing the quantity N (Jaeger (1989)). In a steady state the budget constraint, from the perspective of the social planner, is given by (38) and the assumptions which were made on the production function.

In a first step the social planner will choose the optimal steady state consumption and capital accumulation pattern for a given n. In a second step the optimal n^* will be determined:

$$\max U(c^1, c^2), \tag{39}$$

$$\text{s.t.} \quad c^1 + \frac{c^2}{(1+n)} = f(k) - (n+\delta)k \qquad c^1, c^2 > 0.$$

By substituting the constraint into the utility function Samuelson (1968) obtains:

$$\max_{k,c^2} U(f(k) - (n+\delta)k - \frac{c^2}{(1+n)}, c^2) \qquad c^1, c^2 > 0. \tag{40}$$

The first order conditions for this problem are given by:

$$f'(k_n) - \delta = n, \tag{41}$$

$$\frac{U_{c^1}(c_n^1, c_n^2)}{U_{c^2}(c_n^1, c_n^2)} = (1+n), \tag{42}$$

$$c_n^1 = f(k_n) - (n+\delta)k_n - \frac{c_n^2}{(1+n)}. \tag{43}$$

Condition (43) is a restatement of the steady state budget constraint. Condition (41) is the biological interest rate of Phelps (1961) and condition (42) is the biological interest rate of Samuelson (1958). Together (41) and (42) constitute the two-part golden rule of Samuelson (1968), Phelps (1967a) or Diamond (1965). As Samuelson (1968) and Diamond (1965) point out, the conditions (41) and (42) are independent from each other. This means that the Phelps (1961) biological rate of interest might be violated by a capital intensity which is too high or too low, but at the same time the distribution of consumption between the young and the old generation could satisfy condition (42). Alternatively, the capital intensity can be at k_n and the condition (41) will hold, but by a wrong allocation between the generations condition (42) can be violated.

Conditions (41)-(43) implicitly define the optimal values c_n^1, c_n^2 and k_n, with n as a reminder that these values depend on the growth rate of population. Substituting these optimal values into the utility function gives an indirect utility function:

$$U(n) = U(c_n^1, c_n^2). \tag{44}$$

The next step is to determine the optimal growth rate of population. The optimal n^* can be identified by the first derivative of the maximum value utility function $U(n)$ with respect to n. Hence the problem is:

$$\max_n U\Big(f(k_n) - (n+\delta)k_n - \frac{c_n^2}{(1+n)}, c_n^2\Big). \tag{45}$$

The first order condition is given by:[23]

$$\begin{aligned}\frac{dU}{dn} &= U_{c^1}\Big((f'(k_n) - (n+\delta))\frac{dk}{dn}\Big) \\ &+ U_{c^1}\Big(-k_n + \frac{c_n^2}{(1+n)^2} - \frac{1}{(1+n)}\frac{dc^2}{dn}\Big) + U_{c^2}\frac{dc^2}{dn} = 0.\end{aligned} \tag{46}$$

Using the conditions (41) and (42), condition (46) degenerates into:

$$-k_n + \frac{c_n^2}{(1+n)^2} = 0. \tag{47}$$

Solving for $(1+n)$ yields:

$$1 + n^* = \sqrt{\frac{c_n^2}{k_n}}. \tag{48}$$

Together, conditions (41)-(43) and (47) implicitly define the optimum optimorum with the optimal values c^{1*}, c^{2*}, k^* and n^*. This is the best of all the two-part golden rule steady states which were characterized by the conditions (41)-(43).

In condition (47) both effects can be recognized which were isolated in the two previous sections. In the consumption-loan model we found $\frac{c_n^2}{(1+n)^2}$ in the first order condition (7) for optimal n^*. The other element $-k_n$ was found to be the first derivative (cf. (34)) of per capita consumption with respect to the growth rate of population in the Solow model.

[23]Since $U(n)$ is a maximum value function, we could also use the Envelope theorem (Chiang and Wainwright (2005), pp. 428-441) and obtain (47) right away.

Thus, now there is a tradeoff between the advantages and disadvantages associated with high (low) population growth rates.

An increase in the growth rate of population skews the age distribution permanently in favor of the productive ages, as in the consumption-loan model. The negative effect stems from the need to waste additional resources on capital widening. Diagram 4 gives a graphical exposition of this tradeoff. Choosing n and k influences the slope *and* the horizontal intercept of the availability constraint. The two-part golden rule is satisfied in all three cases **A, B, C** and at $n = n^*$ we reach the highest indifference curve in **A**, the optimum optimorum.

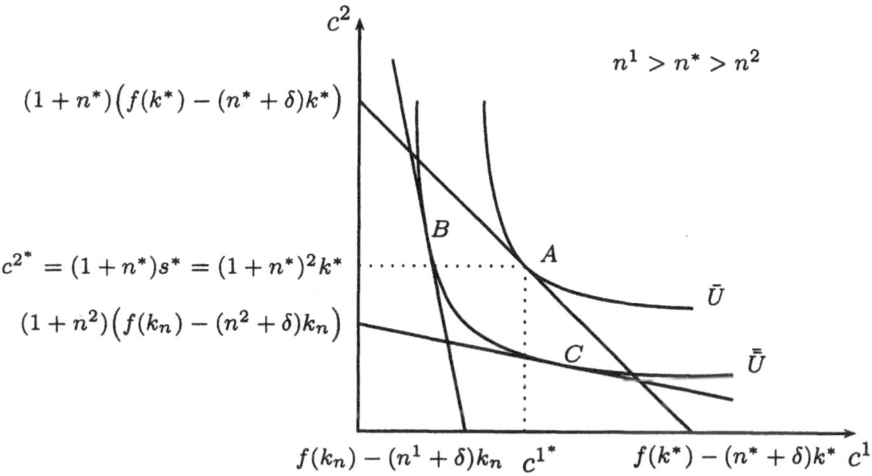

Diagram 4: *Utility in three different steady states, which satisfy the two-part golden rule.*

Following Samuelson (1975a), (p. 536)

However, due to the general nature of the conditions (41)-(43) and (47) there are three problems which can arise:

1. The first order conditions might not all hold with equality, which would imply a corner solution.

2. Multiple solutions might occur.

3. If the first order conditions held with equality, the second order sufficient conditions would have to be checked.

In the following, it will be assumed that the first order conditions actually define one interior solution and the second order conditions will be checked.[24] The result will be that they are not satisfied in general. In order to examine the problems stated above, the special case of a CES utility and production function will be briefly outlined following Michel and Pestieau (1993).

2.3.3. The Second Order Sufficient Conditions

If an inner solution to the problem at hand is assumed, the values c^{1*}, c^{2*}, k^* and n^*, which were implicitly defined by the first order conditions (41)-(43) and (47), characterize a stationary point. In order to find out whether the stationary point is a (local or global) maximum, a minimum or a saddle point, the second order sufficient conditions have to be examined. In a first step we will examine the second order conditions by checking the leading principal minors of the Hessian determinant. It will turn out that the second order conditions for a local maximum are

[24] The treatment of the CES case by Michel and Pestieau (1993) reveals that the first order conditions are satisfied most of the time and that corner solutions and multiple solutions are rather rare.

only satisfied for the two-part golden rule which was characterized by the necessary conditions (41) and (42).

The sufficient condition for an extremum hinges on the sign of the second order total differential of the objective function (Chiang and Wainwright (2005), pp. 297-300). This sign can be determined by checking the definiteness of the Hessian determinant (Chiang and Wainwright (2005), pp. 313-315).

The sufficient condition for a local maximum (minimum) is that the Hessian determinant must be negative (positive) definite around the stationary point (Chiang and Wainwright (2005), (p. 319)).[25] The definiteness of a determinant can be checked by examining the signs of the principal leading minors. The condition for negative definiteness is given by:[26]

$$|H_1| < 0; \quad |H_2| > 0; \quad |H_3| < 0; \quad .....(-1)^n |H_n| > 0. \tag{49}$$

The condition for positive definiteness is given by:

$$|H_1| > 0; \quad |H_2| > 0; \quad |H_3| > 0; \quad .....|H_n| > 0. \tag{50}$$

The objective function to the problem at hand is:

$$\max_{c^2,k,n} U = U\Big(f(k) - (n+\delta)k - \frac{c^2}{(1+n)}, c^2\Big). \tag{51}$$

[25]The sufficient condition for a global maximum (minimum) is that the Hessian determinant must be negative (positive) definite.

[26]Chiang and Wainwright (2005), (p. 317).

Taking into account the first order conditions (41)-(42) and (47), we find that the corresponding Hessian matrix becomes:[27]

$$H = \begin{pmatrix} U_{c^2c^2} - \frac{2}{1+n}U_{c^1c^2} + \frac{1}{(1+n)^2}U_{c^1c^1} & 0 & \frac{1}{(1+n)^2}U_{c^1} \\ 0 & f''(k)U_{c^1} & -U_{c^1} \\ \frac{1}{(1+n)^2}U_{c^1} & -U_{c^1} & -\frac{2c^2}{(1+n)^3}U_{c^1} \end{pmatrix}$$

The leading minors are:

$$|H_1| = U_{c^2c^2} - \frac{2}{1+n}U_{c^1c^2} + \frac{1}{(1+n)^2}U_{c^1c^1} < 0, \tag{52}$$

$$|H_2| = U_{c^1}f''(k)|H_1| > 0, \tag{53}$$

$$|H_3| = -|H_2|U_{c^1}\frac{2c^2}{(1+n)^3} - \frac{1}{(1+n)^4}U_{c^1}^3 f''(k) - U_{c^1}^2|H_1| \lesseqgtr 0. \tag{54}$$

Since the Hessian determinant is indefinite around the stationary point, the conditions for a local maximum are not generally satisfied. Depending on the parameters of the objective function, $|H_3|$ might be negative or positive. If $|H_3|$ was positive, c^{1*}, c^{2*}, k^* and n^* would define a true local maximum.

However, there is one piece of information which can be obtained at this point. The signs of $|H_1|$ and $|H_2|$ indicate that the two-part golden rule characterized by the conditions (41)-(42) in fact satisfies the second order sufficient conditions for a true local maximum. Hence the problem of an indefinite Hessian determinant originates from the additional choice variable n (Samuelson (1975a), p. 534).[28]

---

[27] The bordered Hessian to this problem is given in Appendix A

[28] Phelps (1967a), (pp. 180-181), who also considers the pleasures of parenthood makes a similar but less clear point.

2.3.4. The Special Case of CES Utility and Production Functions

The following is based on the analysis carried out by Michel and Pestieau (1993). They proved that in the framework of CES production and utility functions there does indeed exist an optimal interior solution to the problem stated above, granted that the respective elasticities of substitution are not too large.

The advantage of the CES function is that it is far more general than the Cobb-Douglas or the fixed coefficient functions (which are special cases of the CES function). Thus the technical part of the discussion between Deardorff (1976) and Samuelson (1976) concerning the optimality of c^{1*}, c^{2*}, k^* and n^* will be contained as one element of the more general CES framework.

Recent econometric analysis conducted by de Abreu Pessoa et al. (2005), (p. 35) suggests that the elasticity of substitution between capital and labor τ lies around $0,7$. Using estimates[29] of the Deutsche Bundesbank, Feess (1997), (p. 122) calculates $\tau = 0,8$ for Germany. Arrow et al. (1961), (p. 246) also suggest that τ is probably less than unity. For the elasticity of intertemporal substitution there is still much controversy concerning the appropriate method to estimate σ. According to Guvenen (2002), (p. 27) and Ogaki and Reinhart (1998), (p. 1095) the elasticity of intertemporal substitution may lie between $0,32 - 0,5$

[29]The estimates are based on data from 1970-1994.

and thus much higher than previous estimates ($\sigma = 0,1$) suggested.[30][31] Hence the subcase with $\tau < 1$ and $\sigma < 1$ will be presented here in some detail.

The CES production function in its intensive form is given by:[32]

$$f(k) = A(b + k^{1-\frac{1}{\tau}})^{\frac{\tau}{(\tau-1)}}. \quad (55)$$

The elasticity of substitution τ indicates whether capital and labor are substitutes ($\tau > 1$) or complements ($\tau < 1$). The efficiency parameter $A(> 0)$ represents part of the technology, and the parameter $b(> 0)$ is related to the relative weight of the two input factors capital and labor.

The linear homogenous CES utility function is given by:[33]

$$U(c^1, c^2) = \left((c^1)^{1-\frac{1}{\sigma}} + \beta(c^2)^{1-\frac{1}{\sigma}}\right)^{\frac{\sigma}{\sigma-1}}. \quad (56)$$

The constant elasticity of intertemporal substitution is σ. It indicates how difficult the substitution of current and future consumption is. A time discount factor is represented by $\beta(> 0)$. The assumption that the utility function is linear homogenous implies homothetic preferences.[34]

---

[30] It is obvious that another three-fold increase in these estimates would lead to $\sigma > 1$. Guvenen (2002) also notes that calibrated macroeconomic models designed to match growth and business cycle facts typically require that the IES be close to one.

[31] Samuelson (1976), (p. 521) gives various reasons why the elasticity of substitution should not remain constant while the capital intensity changes with the growth rate of population.

[32] The properties and implications of a CES production function are discussed in Barro and Sala-I-Martin (1995), (pp. 42-46). The CES function was introduced by Arrow et al. (1961).

[33] The properties and implications of a CES or CIES utility function are discussed in Barro and Sala-I-Martin (1995), (pp. 64-65).

[34] Homotheticity and the implications of homothetic utility functions on consumer behavior are discussed in Gravelle and Rees (1992), (pp. 127-128).

As the previous treatment of the sufficient conditions suggested and as Deardorff (1976) showed within a Cobb-Douglas framework, the key problem is the choice of the optimal growth rate for population. Hence the crucial point is the derivative of the indirect utility function (44) with respect to n. As in Michel and Pestieau (1993), we will assume total deprecation in one period, i.e. $\delta = 1$, and define $g := 1 + n$.

As previously derived, the formal problem is to maximize the indirect utility function:

$$\max_g U(g) = U(c_g^1, c_g^2) \tag{57}$$

$$\text{s.t.} \qquad c_g^1 + \frac{c_g^2}{g} = y(g) = (f(k_g) - gk_g).$$

By taking advantage of the homothetic preferences implied by the linear homogenous utility function (56), it is possible to separate the negative effect of capital widening and the positive effect of an increased interest rate on savings. The indirect utility can be expressed by:

$$V(g) = \varphi(g)y(g). \tag{58}$$

In equation (58), $y(g)$ is the per capita output which is negatively depending on the need for capital widening. The other element in (58), $\varphi(g) := Max_c U(c^1, g(1 - c^1))$, gives the utility level per each unit of income which is, due to the increased interest, positively depending on g.[35]

For elasticities of substitution $\sigma > 0$ and $\sigma \neq 1$, the utility function $\varphi(g)$ takes on the following form:[36]

$$\varphi(g) = (1 + \beta^\sigma g^{\sigma-1})^{\frac{1}{\sigma-1}}. \tag{59}$$

[35]The capital Max indicates that $Max_c^1 U(c^1, g(1 - c^1))$ is a maximum value function.

[36]Michel and Pestieau (1993) derive $\varphi(g)$ and $y(g)$ in their appendix (pp. 357-359).

For elasticities of substitution $\tau > 0$ and $\tau \neq 1$, the per capita income $y(g)$ is:

$$y(g) = \left(\frac{1}{b}\right)^{\frac{\tau}{1-\tau}} A\left(1 - \left(\frac{g}{A}\right)^{(1-\tau)}\right)^{\frac{1}{1-\tau}}. \tag{60}$$

In the case of $\tau < 1$, the technical parameter A must be greater than g in order to allow for positive per capita output. However, the crucial implication of $\tau < 1$ stems from the fact that there is now a finite upper boundary for the per capita output, which means that, contrary to the Inada conditions, $f(\infty) < \infty$. For elasticities $\tau \geqq 1$ there is no upper boundary for the per capita output and we have $f(\infty) = \infty$.

Inserting the equations (59) and (60) into (58) yields:

$$V(g) = \left((1 + \beta^{\sigma} g^{\sigma-1})^{\frac{1}{(\sigma-1)}}\right)\left((\frac{1}{b})^{\frac{\tau}{1-\tau}} A\left(1 - \left(\frac{g}{A}\right)^{(1-\tau)}\right)^{\frac{1}{1-\tau}}\right). \tag{61}$$

In order to obtain an expression for $V'(g)$, which is accessible for interpretation, the next two steps are to take the natural logarithm of $V(g)$ and differentiate it with respect to g. Taking the natural logarithm gives:

$$ln(V(g)) = \frac{1}{(\sigma - 1)} ln\left((1 + \beta^{\sigma} g^{\sigma-1})\right)$$

$$+ \frac{1}{1-\tau} ln\left(1 - (\frac{g}{A})^{1-\tau}\right) + constant. \tag{62}$$

Differentiation with respect to g yields:

$$\frac{V'(g)}{V(g)} = \frac{\beta^{\sigma} g^{\sigma-2}}{1 + \beta^{\sigma} g^{\sigma-1}} - \frac{g^{-\tau}}{A^{1-\tau} - g^{1-\tau}}. \tag{63}$$

From (63) a function $G(g)$ can be derived, which has the same sign as $V'(g)$:

$$G(g) = A^{1-\tau} - 2g^{1-\tau} - \beta^{-\sigma} g^{2-\sigma-\tau}. \tag{64}$$

Due to the assumptions $\tau < 1$ and $\sigma < 1$, G exhibits the following properties, which ensure that there is one optimal interior solution where $g = g^* = 1 + n^*$:

$$G(0) > 0; \qquad G(A) < 0; \qquad G'(g) < 0; \qquad g \in (0, A). \tag{65}$$

The treatment of all other possible cases lead Michel and Pestieau to the results which are summarized in Table 1[37]:

Table 1: **Existence of an interior optimum growth rate for population for the CES/CEIS economy**

CES/CEIS	$\sigma < 1$	$\sigma = 1$	$\sigma > 1$
$\tau < 1$	yes	yes	yes
$\tau = 1$	yes	no	no
$\tau > 1$	no	no	no

Source: Michel and Pestieau (1993), (p. 357)

According to Table 1, low elasticities of substitution of capital and labor typically lead to an interior solution, which is an optimum. The elasticity of intertemporal substitution in the utility function is only of importance in two cases, $(\tau < 1; \sigma > 1)$ and $(\tau = 1; \sigma < 1)$. The case of $(\tau < 1; \sigma < 1)$ satisfies the conditions for an interior maximum.

[37]For the case $\tau < 1, \sigma > 1$, either A has to be large enough or $\sigma < 2 - \tau$. In the case of $\tau = 1, \sigma < 1$ $f(k) = k^\alpha$, it is necessary that $\alpha < 0,5$.

The Cobb-Douglas case ($\tau = 1; \sigma = 1$), which was already treated by Deardorff (1976), satisfies the conditions for an interior minimum. Concerning the Deardorff (1976) comment there is one point to note: The claim that "the result in the Cobb-Douglas case is hardly pathological" (Deardorff (1976), p. 514) seems to be wrong. Due to the high elasticity of substitution of one, there is no upper boundary for the per capita output in the Cobb-Douglas case, and this is what makes a corner solution with $n^* = -\delta$, $f'(\infty) = 0$ and $f(\infty) = \infty$ possible.

The only point missing here is the fixed coefficient case ($\tau = 0; \sigma = 0$) brought up by Samuelson (1976), which is not an element of Table 1. In the fixed coefficient case with a technically determined capital intensity, the existence of an interior optimum depends on the relative weight of current and future consumption and the capital labor ratio. For a low capital intensity and a relatively high weight of old age consumption an optimal intermediate n^* exists. Hence the previous discussion can be summarized in Diagram 5 as follows: There is a positive effect (1) and a negative effect (2) stemming from an increase in the growth rate of population that overlay each other in a way, which, depending on the structure of the economy, allows for an intermediate maximum or minimum.

Having said that there probably does exist an optimum growth rate implies by no means that this is a feasible rate for economic policy. The fact that there might be a (biological) minimum n^{min} or maximum n^{max} feasible rate of population growth never appeared in the previous discussion. Another objection may lie in the fact that even if the growth rate was an ordinary policy variable, it would still take "a period of

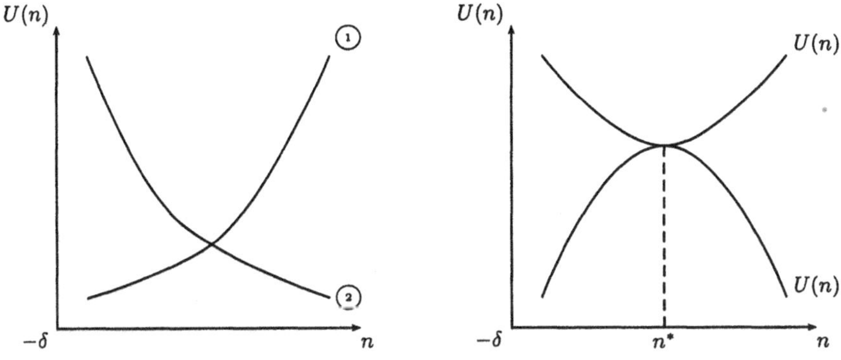

Diagram 5: *The tradeoff between capital widening and intergenerational transfers.*

Following Samuelson (1976), (pp. 517-518)

time equal to the human life span to get the (desired) age distribution of the population" (Phelps (1967a), p. 183). Taking into account these limitations, it might still turn out that $n^* < n^{min}$ and that population should still decline as fast as possible or that the growth rate should not be changed at all due to the costs which might be associated with the period of transition.

On the other side, one might argue that if the growth rate of population changed mostly for exogenous reasons, the previous analysis would at least reveal the long-run consequences and whether such a change in fertility should be encouraged or not.

However, the properties of the social optimum lead to the result that there probably is an interior optimum; the next question is whether or not such an optimum can be reached and sustained.

2.3.5. Attainability and Stability of the Social Optimum: the Serendipity Theorem

The previous discussion of the social optimum was concerned with the question: How much capital should be accumulated and how should the resources available for consumption in each period be distributed among the generations? The answer to this question was the two-part golden rule, which was characterized by the conditions (41) and (42).

Once the optimal consumption and accumulation pattern were found, the optimum optimorum was derived by setting the growth rate of population to a level where individual steady state utility was maximized. The first order condition for the optimal n^* was given by (47).

In the following, the question will be examined whether such a social optimum is sustainable once it is reached, without interference by the government.

In order to investigate this matter it is necessary to compare the competitive laissez faire equilibrium with the social optimum.

Individual Utility Maximization: As in Diamond (1965), the representative individual lives for two periods. In the first period, each individual supplies one unit of labor inelastically and receives an income which amounts to the real wage. This income is used on first period consumption, and savings for the period of retirement. The savings of period t are the capital which is used to produce output in period $t+1$. This means that the aggregate productive capital in period $t+1$ in the economy is equal to the aggregate savings of the retired generation. At the end of the second period of life, each individual consumes his savings plus the interest. This leads to the following individual maximization problem:

$$\max_{c_t^1, c_{t+1}^2} U(c_t^1, c_{t+1}^2) \tag{66}$$

$$s.t. \qquad c_t^1 + s_t = w_t; \qquad c_{t+1}^2 = (1 + r_{t+1})s_t.$$

The wages and the real interest rate $r_{t+1} - \delta$ earned on capital depend on the respective marginal products according to (19) and (20). Due to the factor-prices, which are fully flexible, the factor markets are always in an equilibrium (Blanchard and Fischer (1989), pp. 91-98).

Goods Market Equilibrium: The goods market is in an equilibrium when the planned net investment equals the planned net savings:

$$K_{t+1} - K_t = N_t s(w_t, r_{t+1}) - K_t. \tag{67}$$

Eliminating K_t, which is the dissaving of the old generation, and dividing with N_t gives the alternative equilibrium condition:

$$(1 + n)k_{t+1} = s_t(w_t; r_{t+1}); \qquad 0 < s_w < 1; \qquad s_r \lesseqgtr 0. \tag{68}$$

The assumption of $0 < s_w < 1$ implies that current and future consumption are normal goods (Diamond (1965), p. 1131). The sign of s_r is ambiguous due to the different directions of income and substitution effect (Blanchard and Fischer (1989), pp. 93-94). Equation (68) describes the dynamic behavior of the capital stock and gives rise to:

$$\frac{dk_{t+1}}{dk_t} = \frac{-s_w \tilde{k} f''(\tilde{k})}{1 + n - s_r f''(\tilde{k})}. \tag{69}$$

With $\tilde{k}$ being the steady state value of k.

In accordance with Blanchard and Fischer (1989), (pp. 91-98), we will "simply assume" that there exists one unique asymptotically (for the case of oscillatory stability see Appendix C) stable steady state equilibrium. This assumption implies:

$$0 < \frac{-s_w \tilde{k} f''(\tilde{k})}{1 + n - s_r f''(\tilde{k})} < 1. \tag{70}$$

In such a steady state equilibrium, the capital intensity, the per capita income, the real wage and the real interest rate remain constant over time. A constant capital intensity requires, according to the goods market equilibrium condition (68), that the private savings of the old generation have to be just sufficient to equip the young generation with enough capital to keep k constant, which means:

$$(1 + n)k = s(w, r) = \frac{c^2}{1 + r - \delta}. \tag{71}$$

Comparison of the Individual Behavior and the Social Optimum:[38] The individual utility maximization problem (66) leads to the following first order conditions:

$$\frac{U_{c^1}}{U_c^2} = 1 + r - \delta, \tag{72}$$

$$w = f(k) - f'(k)k = c^1 + \frac{c^2}{1 + r - \delta}. \tag{73}$$

If it is assumed that the economy starts with a capital intensity of k_n where $f'(k_n) = n + \delta$, the first order conditions (72) and (73) coincide with the conditions (42) and (43) for the two-part golden rule, and

[38]In this paragraph we will try to verbalize the meaning of the Serendipity Theorem. From the formal perspective it is obvious that for c^{1*}, c^{2*}, k^*, n^* conditions (41), (42), (43), (47), (71), (72) and (73) hold simultaneously. For $n \neq n^*$ (compare (47) and (71)) this is not the case.

the representative individual would choose a consumption pattern where $c^1 = c_n^1$, $c^2 = c_n^2$. Inserting these values into the goods market steady state equilibrium condition (71) gives:

$$(1+n)k_n = s(w,r) = \frac{c_n^2}{1+r-\delta} = \frac{c_n^2}{1+n}. \tag{74}$$

This equation, however, is equal to the first order condition (47) for the optimal growth rate of population, which is only satisfied if $n = n^*$. Hence the social optimum optimorum is a feasible laissez faire steady state allocation. This is the Serendipity Theorem discerned by Samuelson: "At the optimum growth rate n^*, private lifetime saving will just support the most-golden golden-rule lifetime state" (Samuelson (1975a), p. 535). Due to the assumption of one unique steady state equilibrium, this also means that at $n = n^*$ the economy will automatically evolve into the most golden golden rule steady state, the optimum optimorum.

In all other cases where $n \neq n^*$ the social optimum characterized by the two-part golden rule is not compatible with the individual behavior, since at a capital intensity of k_n, the steady state goods market equilibrium condition is violated. This means that at k_n the private life-cycle saving will not just support the two-part golden rule steady state. Hence, the government would have to intervene in order to restore optimality in an economy where $n \neq n^*$ by introducing some sort of social security system as described by Samuelson (1975b).[39] The Serendipity Theorem is illustrated in Diagram 4 where $c^{2*} = (1+n^*)^2k^*$. In the following

[39]The basic idea in this essay is to accumulate "social capital" in the case of under-accumulation, which can be held constant through the investing of profits. In the case of over-accumulation, the government introduces an unfunded social security system (Samuelson (1975b), pp. 541-542).

discussion we will not label all optimal variables with a " $*$ ". According to the Serendipity Theorem, we can abbreviate our formal expressions and refer to *the* allocation at $n = n^*$.

2.3.6. The Optimum Growth Rate for Population in a Laissez Faire Economy

The previous summary of the discussion between Samuelson, Deardorff, and Michel and Pestieau focused on the optimum growth rate of population in an economy where a fully-informed social planner can choose all quantities such that the economy is in a steady state where the individual utility is maximized. If there does indeed exist an interior solution which defines a truly optimal growth rate of population, the following discussion will be, due to the Serendipity Theorem, worthless from the normative perspective. In all other cases, i.e. no interior optimum, or an optimal growth rate n^* which is so low that it cannot be reached, the following discussion of the laissez faire equilibria seems to make sense.

In a second article, Samuelson (1975b) showed that if the growth rate of population differed from the optimal level, a social security system would be necessary to reach a steady state where the two-part golden rule would be satisfied. Diagram 6 indicates that, depending on the structure of the economy, such a social security system would have to be over- or under-funded in order to reach the optimal capital intensity k_n.

This discussion leaves at least one question untouched: What is the optimum growth rate of population in a laissez faire economy where there is no authority which can accumulate enough capital via a social security system such that the two-part golden rule is always satisfied?

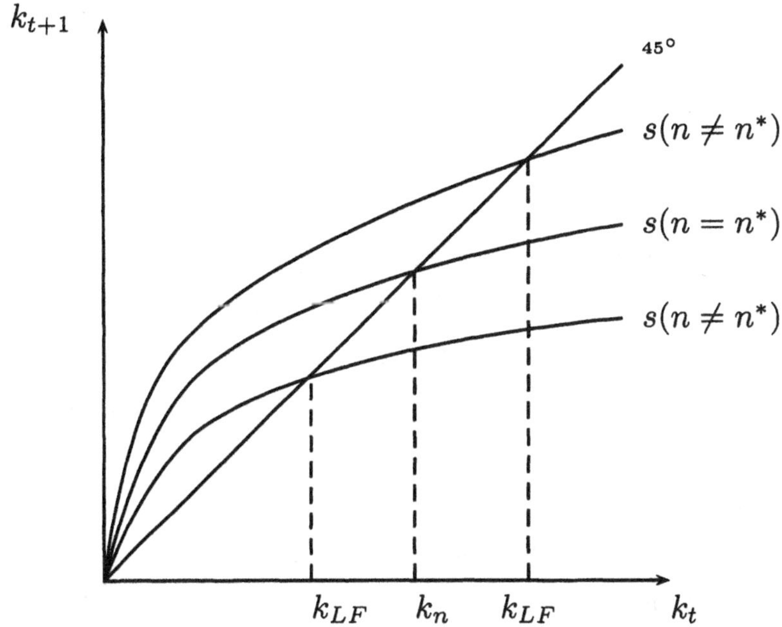

Diagram 6: *For growth rates $n \neq n^*$ individual savings do not allow for golden rule growth.*

We will therefore reconsider the n^* of Samuelson (1975a) in a laissez faire framework.

The reason to examine this question basically stems from two very basic insights into the nature of a social optimum: In theory the social optimum is always as good as or, in the case of some sort of market failure, better than the laissez faire equilibrium. In the real world, however, a social planner who tries to control all quantities is usually a catastrophe or at least a (heavy) burden for everybody involved, and a government which accumulates capital via a social security system at a scale that helps to notably increase the capital intensity seems to be like, to use Samuelson's words, an egg which stands upon its end.[40]

This means that in the case of the optimum growth rate for population the knowledge of the location of the best laissez faire equilibrium might be worth a lot more than some social optimum, apart from $n = n^*$, which can never be reached. Hence the crucial point is that the $U(n)$ curve derived by Samuelson and Deardorff is an indirect utility function originating from the two-part golden rule. In their discussion of the social optimum, however, the problem that the two-part golden rule needs to be supplemented by some social security system to remain valid once $n \neq n^*$ was not discussed. Since there appears to be no literature on this subject, the intention with the following considerations is to supplement the foregoing discussion.

In order to examine whether n^* is the optimum growth rate in a laissez faire economy, it is necessary to make a clear distinction between the laissez faire equilibria and the planned equilibria.

As already stated, the laissez faire equilibrium is characterized by the following equations:[41]

$$\frac{U_{c^1}}{U_{c^2}} = 1 + f'(k), \tag{75}$$

$$f(k) - kf'(k) = c^1 + \frac{c^2}{1 + f'(k)}, \tag{76}$$

$$c^2 = (1 + f'(k))(1 + n)k, \tag{77}$$

[40] Another suggestion in Samuelson (1975b), (p. 543), is that the social planner shall maximize a "true" utility function $v(c^1, c^2)$, which differs from the one upon which people act.

[41] From now on we will no longer account for the rate of deprecation explicitly since it always remains constant. Thus $f(k)$ will be net output and $f'(k)$ will be the net interest rate as in Samuelson (1975a).

$$s = (1+n)k = \frac{c^2}{1+f'(k)}. \tag{78}$$

The first three equations characterize all possible laissez faire equilibria and implicitly define the steady state values $c^1(n)$, $c^2(n)$ and $k(n)$. Equation (78) is only a reminder of the life-cycle savings condition and the relation between old age consumption and the capital intensity.

Along the lines of equations (75)-(77) and the previous discussion of the social optimum the different sets of equilibria which can arise are given in Diagram 7:

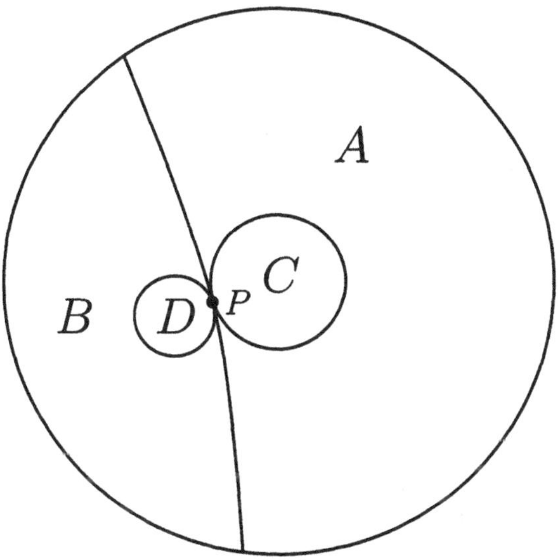

Diagram 7: *The problem of optimal population decomposed into sets and subsets.*

Set **A** contains all equilibria which satisfy the budget or availability constraint (38) of the economy. Set **B** contains all equilibria where the individual budget constraint (76) and the life-cycle savings condition (77) are satisfied. Set **C** contains all planned steady states which satisfy the two-part golden rule. Set **D** contains all laissez faire steady states where the individual consumption pattern (75) is compatible with equations (76) and (77). According to the Serendipity Theorem, there is only one equilibrium at $n = n^*$ where individual utility maximization coincides with the social optimum; this equilibrium is indicated by point **P**.[42]

In order to derive some qualitative results on the nature of the problem at hand, it will be useful to display these sets in a r, n diagram. Hence it is necessary to gather information on the sign of $\frac{dk}{dn}$, since we need to determine the sign of $\frac{dr}{dn}$. Total differentiation of equation system (75)-(77) yields, using Cramer's rule, an ambiguous sign for $\frac{dk}{dn}$.[43] However, according to the assumption made on stability, condition (70) can be used to derive $\frac{dk}{dn} < 0$ (Blanchard and Fischer (1989), p. 96), which implies $\frac{dr}{dn} > 0$.[44] This means that we have:

$$\frac{dr}{dn} = f''(k(n))\frac{dk}{dn} > 0. \tag{79}$$

The sets **C** and **D** can now be displayed in a r, n diagram:

---

[42]The element of the Serendipity Theorem, which states the equality of the planned and the laissez faire equilibrium, is valid regardless of whether the first order condition for n^* defines the best or worst of all planned steady states.

[43]From the formal perspective, this is the same problem as in Samuelson (1941), (pp. 113-117).

[44]Total differentiation of (68) leads to $\frac{dk}{dn} = \frac{\frac{-s}{1+n}}{(1+n)+s_w kf''-s_r f''}$, which is negative by virtue of condition (70); according to condition (70) we have $(1+n)+s_w kf''-s_r f'' > 0$, i.e. the denominator is positive and the numerator is negative as long as savings (and thus the capital intensity) are positive. The oscillatory case, where the sufficient conditions for an interior optimum are always satisfied, will be treated separately in Appendix C.

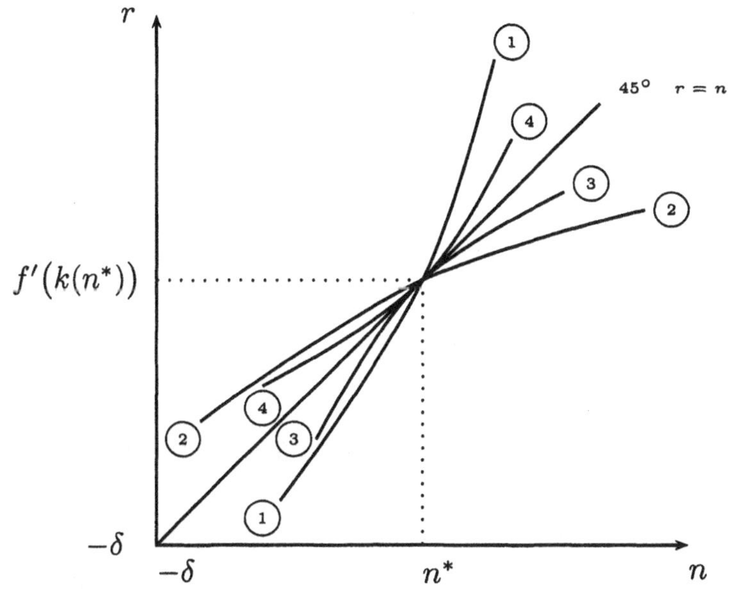

Diagram 8: *The crucial r-n relation.*

Diagram 8 displays all planned equilibria **C** on the 45° line where $f'(k) = r = n$. The locus of the laissez faire equilibria **D** is ambiguous; there are a priori four different cases possible. All equilibria below (above) the 45° line are dynamically inefficient (efficient). Since there is only one equilibrium **P** where the planned economy and the laissez faire economy lead to an identical allocation, Diagram 8 reveals the following theorem:

Theorem 1: *For a laissez faire economy a change in the growth rate of population can only shift the economy from dynamic efficiency (inefficiency) to dynamic inefficiency (efficiency) at the pivotal point* ***P*** *where* $n = n^*$.

According to Table 2, there are four cases which have to be distinguished.

Table 2: **Marginal utility and efficiency**

Case	$n < n^*$	$n = n^*$	$n > n^*$
1	$f' < n; U'(n) > 0$	$f' = n; U'(n) = 0$	$f' > n; U'(n) < 0$
2	$f' > n; U'(n) < 0$	$f' = n; U'(n) = 0$	$f' < n; U'(n) > 0$
3	$f' < n; U'(n) > 0$	$f' = n; U'(n) = 0$	$f' < n; U'(n) > 0$
4	$f' > n; U'(n) < 0$	$f' = n; U'(n) = 0$	$f' > n; U'(n) < 0$

After these preparations it is now possible to show the condition under which $n = n^*$ ensures an optimum in a laissez faire economy. According to equations (75)-(77), the formal problem of finding the laissez faire optimum growth rate of population is given by:[45]

$$\begin{aligned} \max_n U(n) &= U\Big(f(k) - kf'(k) - (1+n)k, (1+f'(k))(1+n)k\Big); \\ k &= k(n). \end{aligned}$$

The first order condition for the optimum growth rate is:

$$\begin{aligned} \frac{dU}{dn} &= U_{c^1}\Big[\Big(-f''(k)k - (1+n)\Big)\frac{dk}{dn} - k\Big] \\ &+ U_{c^2}\Big(f''(k)(1+n)k + (1+f'(k))(1+n)\Big)\frac{dk}{dn} \\ &+ U_{c^2}(1+f'(k))k = 0. \end{aligned} \tag{80}$$

[45]It is important to note that in the framework of a laissez fair economy the representative individual benefits from high growth rates of population, because he receives a higher interest on his private savings, which makes future consumption cheaper. With the exception of the equilibrium at $n = n^*$, this is a different channel and a different magnitude than the one we observed in the planned economy.

The use of (75), which is always satisfied in a laissez faire economy, and rearrangement of (80) gives:

$$\frac{dU}{dn} = U_{c^1}\left[\frac{n - f'(k)}{1 + f'(k)} f''(k)k\right]\frac{dk}{dn} = 0. \tag{81}$$

Condition (81) reveals that the sign of $\frac{dU}{dn}$ hinges on the sign of $n - f'(k)$:

Theorem 2: *In the case of dynamic inefficiency or over-accumulation an increase in* n *increases per capita utility, and, in the case of dynamic efficiency an increase in* n *decreases per capita utility.*

This is summarized in Table 2 and illustrated in Diagram 9. At $f'(k) = n(= n^*)$ (this is point **P** in Diagram 7) the first order condition is satisfied.

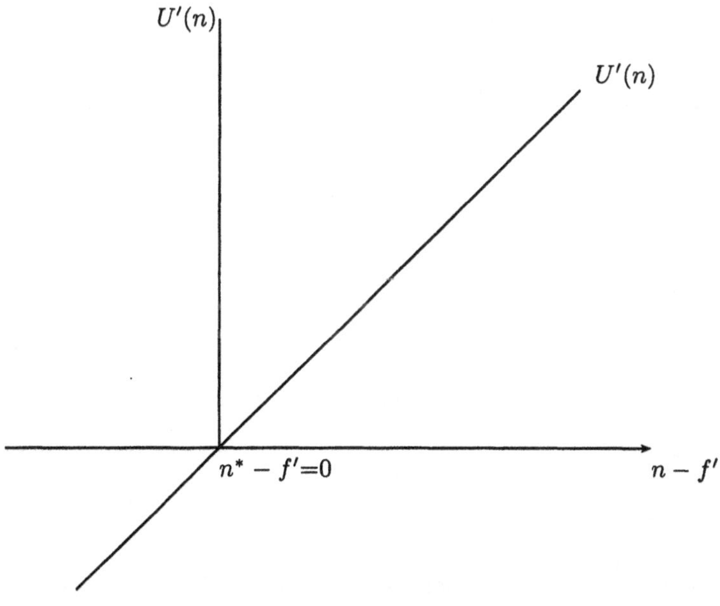

Diagram 9: *Marginal utility and efficiency.*

The second derivative which describes the curvature of $U(n)$ is given by:[46]

$$\begin{aligned}
\frac{d^2U}{dn^2} &= U_{c^1}\Big[\frac{(1+f')(1-f''\frac{dk}{dn})-(n-f')f''\frac{dk}{dn}}{(1+f')^2}f''k\Big]\frac{dk}{dn} \\
&+ U_{c^1}\frac{(n-f')}{1+f'}\Big[(f'''k+f'')(\frac{dk}{dn})^2+f''k\frac{d^2k}{dn^2}\Big] \\
&+ \Big(U_{c^1c^2}\frac{dc^2}{dn}+U_{c^1c^1}\frac{dc^1}{dn}\Big)\Big[\frac{(n-f')}{1+f'}f''k\frac{dk}{dn}\Big] \lesseqqgtr 0. \qquad (82)
\end{aligned}$$

Since we already know that there is only one pivotal point where four cases can be distinguished, it is most important to examine the sign of (82) at this point. With $f'(k) = n^*$, (82) becomes:

$$\frac{d^2U}{dn^2} = U_{c^1}\Big[\frac{(1-f''\frac{dk}{dn})}{(1+f')}f''k\Big]\frac{dk}{dn} \gtreqqless 0. \qquad (83)$$

The graphic exposition in Diagram 8 of the four cases together with (79) indicates that at the pivotal point **P** the sign of (83) differs from case to case:

$$f''\frac{dk}{dn} = \frac{dr}{dn} \gtreqqless 1. \qquad (84)$$

For Case 1 we have, for example, $f''\frac{dk}{dn} = \frac{dr}{dn} > 1$ (the n, r line in Diagram 8 is crossing the 45° line from below). Inserting (84) into (83) reveals that at point **P** we have:

$$\frac{d^2U}{dn^2} < 0.$$

[46]In order to abbreviate the subsequent expressions, we follow Diamond (1965) and define $f' := f'(k)$ and $f'' := f''(k)$. Since the expressions in $\frac{dc^2}{dn}$ and $\frac{dc^1}{dn}$ do not influence the sign of $\frac{d^2U}{dn^2}$ at the stationary point, we do not state them in terms of the capital intensity.

Hence the second order condition for a laissez faire maximum would be satisfied. Thus the formal condition for $\frac{d^2U}{dn^2} < 0$ is $f''\frac{dk}{dn} > 1$. Total differentiation of (78) gives rise to:

$$\frac{dk}{dn} = \frac{\frac{-s}{1+n}}{(1+n) + s_w k f'' - s_r f''}. \tag{85}$$

Multiplying with f'' gives the sufficient condition for the existence of a laissez faire maximum at n^*:

$$f''\frac{dk}{dn} = \frac{\frac{-s}{1+n}}{(1+n)\frac{1}{f''} + s_w k - s_r} = \frac{-k}{(1+n)\frac{1}{f''} + s_w k - s_r} > 1. \tag{86}$$

From condition (86) we can see that the existence of a laissez faire optimum at n^* depends on the structure of the economy, which is embodied in the production and the utility function, which implies the savings behavior.[47] The other three cases can be treated similarly and one can find that at the point **P**: there is an inflection point in the special Cases 3 and 4, and a minimum in Case 2. From the economic perspective, Case 2 does not make much sense since the economy would experience over-accumulation for $n > n^*$ and "under-accumulation" for $n < n^*$. Case 3 with its permanent inefficiency also seems to be not meaningful. Case 4 is rather special, but cannot be ruled out right away from the economic perspective.

Instead of treating the four cases by examining the sign of $\frac{d^2U}{dn^2}$, we can also use the first order condition (81) and Theorem 1 to examine the shape of $U(n)$.

---

[47]The sign of s_r depends on the elasticity of substitution σ; for $\sigma > 1$ the substitution effect dominates the income effect and we have $s_r > 0$ (Blanchard and Fischer (1989), p. 89).

A graphical exposition of the four cases: **Case 1 [left($n < n^*$):1-right($n > n^*$):1], Case 2 [2-2], Case 3 [1-2], Case 4 [2-1]** in Diagram 10 leads to the following conclusion: As in the planned economy, depending on the structure of the economy which is embodied in the production and utility functions, the optimum growth rate can be a boundary solution or an inner optimum/pessimum. The $U(n)$ curve displays a planning minimum at n^* as in Deardorff (1976).

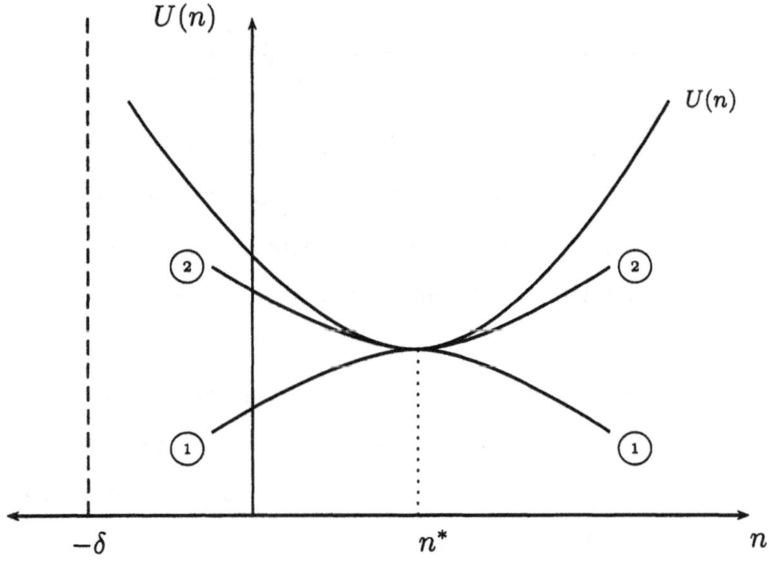

Diagram 10: *Utility and population in a laissez faire economy.*

Interpretation: It was not possible to show that a growth rate of n^* satisfies the conditions for a laissez faire optimum in general. Instead we found a similar picture as in the discussion of the planned economy where it is necessary to recurse to special cases due to the problem that, once more, our general objective function is not concave in (k, c^2, n) together.

Still there are several valuable results concerning the conditions which have to be met in order to allow for an inner laissez faire optimum or a planning optimum:

1. The optimum growth rate of population in a laissez faire economy: Case 1: $n = n^*$ is an interior global optimum; Case 2: n^* is a global minimum; Case 3: in the case of permanent inefficiency n should be as large as possible; Case 4: in the case of permanent efficiency n should be as small as possible.

2. The optimum growth rate of population in a planned economy: Case 1: allows for an interior maximum or minimum at n^*; Case 2: allows only for a minimum at n^* since the laissez faire equilibria cannot provide a higher utility than the social optimum; Case 3: allows only for a minimum at n^*; Case 4: allows only for a minimum at n^*.

At this point it appears necessary to test whether condition (86) holds, for example, in some CES cases with $\sigma \gtrless 1; \tau \gtrless 1$. Such an inquiry will be unnecessary, since the diagrammatic discussion in the next section will reveal that the findings of Michel and Pestieau (1993), i.e. Table 1, remain fully valid in the laissez faire framework.

2.3.7. A Diagrammatic Discussion

This section will contain the essence of the problem – discussed by Samuelson (1975a), Deardorff (1976) and Samuelson (1976) – of optimal population growth in the neoclassical overlapping generations model.[48] There are two main results:

1. The conditions for a laissez faire maximum at n^* are identical to the conditions for a social optimum at n^*. The necessary and sufficient conditions will be given. In Appendix B we will prove the following results.

2. A diagrammatic proof for the optimality of the two-part golden rule allocation.

The first result can be derived by comparing the problem of the social optimum (pessimum) with the laissez faire problem; the laissez faire problem can be summarized in Diagram 11:[49]

[48]A related point can be found in Phelps (1968). Reference to this is being made in Appendix E.

[49]In order to allow for clearness Cases 3 and 4 are omitted. However, the reader can, as in Diagram 10 or 8, construct the curves for Cases 3 and 4 (without adding any lines) in Diagram 11. Cases 3 and 4 lead to an indifference curve that intersects the factor-price frontier at n^*. Omitting the Case of permanent inefficiency seems to be an obvious step. Omitting the case of permanent efficiency (case 4) might be the wrong choice since permanent efficiency in a laissez faire framework without government interference seems to be natural. Case 4 also implies a preference for ever larger wage income, which is close to our results in section 2.2.3..

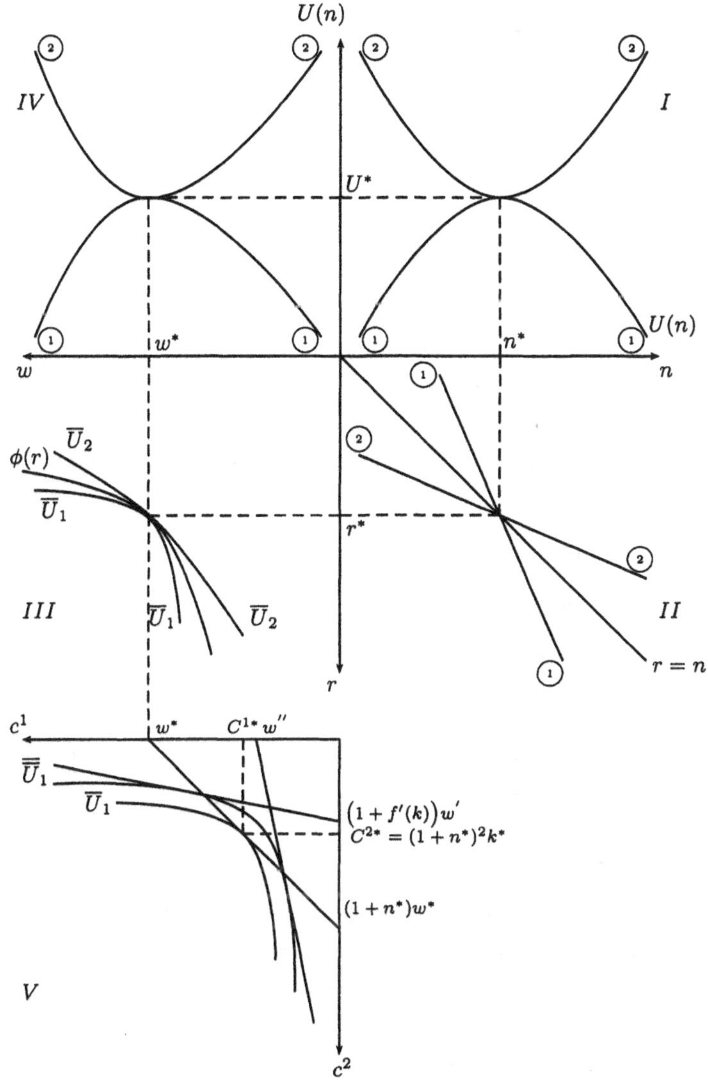

Diagram 11: *A complete representation of the problem of optimal population in the neoclassical overlapping generations model.*

The first quadrant is the familiar U, n diagram (Samuelson (1976), p. 518), the second quadrant is the n, r diagram with $\frac{dk}{dn} < 0$[50], the third quadrant is the w, r diagram of Diamond (Diamond (1965), p. 1140) which contains the convex factor price frontier ϕ and the respective convex indifference curves indicating an optimum (pessimum). The fourth quadrant closes the circle and gives the wage utility relation. The fifth quadrant is the c^1, c^2 diagram (see Diagram 4) of Samuelson (1975a).[51][52]

Diagram 11 makes the following visible: Choosing the growth rate of population means choosing the factor prices, regardless whether we discuss a planned or a laissez faire economy. The crucial points are the indifference curves which illustrate the essential tradeoff between wages and the price of old age consumption. The other aspect is the production technology, which determines the curvature ϕ'' of the factor price frontier.[53] Quadrant III contains basically the same economic content as Quadrant V.

Diagram 11 also indicates that the minimum (Case 2) at n^* clearly hinges on the respective curvature of the indifference curve and the factor price frontier. To allow for a minimum, the representative individual

---

[50]Without further assumptions on the sign of $\frac{d^2r}{dn^2} = f'''(\frac{dk}{dn})^2 + f''\frac{d^2k}{dn^2}$ we cannot determine the shape (concave or convex) of the laissez faire loci in quadrant II. In order to simplify the diagrammatic exposition these loci will be drawn as straight lines from now on.

[51]For reasons of clarity, Quadrant V contains only indifference curves which represent Case 1.

[52]It is obvious that some of the quadrants are redundant, but the idea in this section is to give a diagrammatic summary that makes the interrelations, which were implicit in our formal discussion, entirely visible.

[53]An exposition of the factor-price frontier is given in Jones (1975), (pp. 131-135), Jaeger (1980) and Samuelson (1962).

must have a clear preference for extremes. Alternatively, the curvature of factor-price frontier at k^* would have to be extremely large, i.e. $|f''(k^*)|$ very small.

After the counterintuitive change in efficiency, which was already noted in the foregoing section, these obscure preferences for extremes are a second reason to dismiss Case 2. After all, it appears that the case of a laissez faire pessimum is rather a technical possibility and one might even argue that the minimum at n^* is similar to the meaningless (unstable) steady state with $k = 0$ in the Solow (1956) model.

It is, however, necessary to note that our discussion in the previous section was not explicitly concerned with the tangency of the individual indifference curve and the factor-price frontier. But we can argued that we proved an optimum (pessimum) for Case 1 (2) at n^* and hence there is no other way to arrange the indifference curves in the third quadrant of Diagram 11. In order not to distort our diagrammatic discussion, the formal discussion of this aspect will be given in Appendix B. What we can point out right away is that the first order condition (47) for the existence of an interior n^* can be rearranged:

$$\begin{aligned} -k^* + \frac{c^{2*}}{(1+n^*)^2} &= 0 \quad \Leftrightarrow \quad -k^* = \frac{-s^*}{(1+f'(k(n^*)))}; \\ f'(k(n^*)) &= n^*; \quad c^{2*} = (1+n^*)s^*. \end{aligned} \tag{87}$$

The equations in (87) reveal that the slope of the indifference curve, which is $\frac{-s}{(1+f'(k))}$, must equal the slope of the factor price frontier, which is $-k$, at the optimum growth rate n^* (Diamond (1965), p. 1140).

We can now read the conditions for a laissez faire optimum at n^* from Diagram 11: It is necessary that the indifference curve is a tangent to the factor-price frontier, and it is sufficient that the curvature of the indifference curve is algebraically larger than that of the factor-price frontier. This point will also be proven in Appendix B.

The planning problem can now be summarized in a reduced Diagram 12:

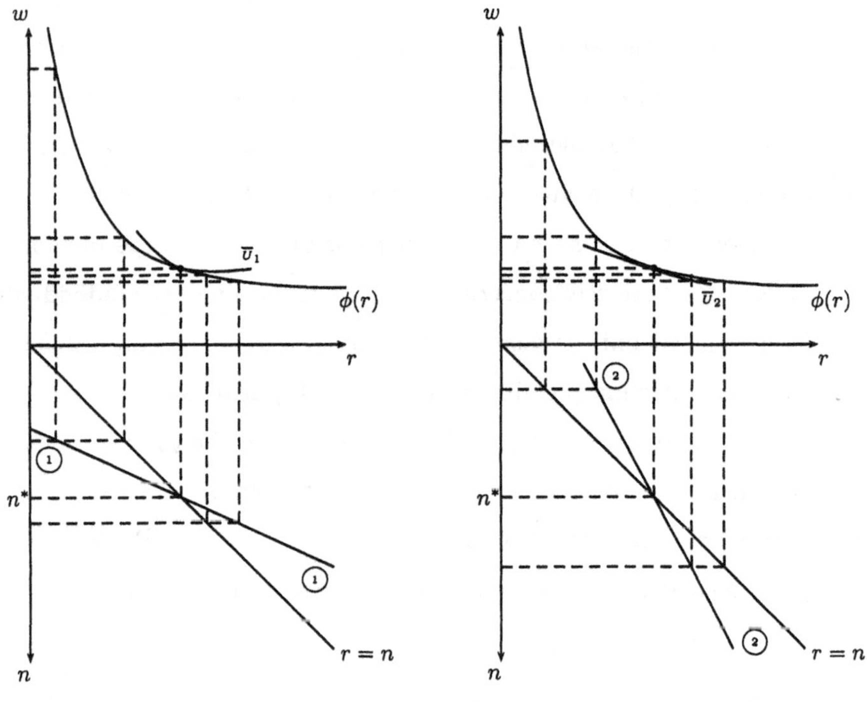

Diagram 12: *A diagrammatic proof for the optimality of the two-part golden rule.*

Diagram 12 treats Case 1 (left) and Case 2 (right) separately. In both cases it is obvious that the two-part golden rule always allows to reach a higher indifference curve than the laissez faire allocation and it reconfirms the finding that the two-part golden rule allocation constitutes a true (local) maximum.[54][55] This is the diagrammatic "proof" that the two-part golden rule allocation is a maximum when compared to the allocation in the competitive economy.

More interesting, however, is the fact that for each and every given growth rate in the planning framework and in the laissez faire framework we are *on the same* factor price frontier (only at a different location), and the question whether we have a planning optimum at n^* boils down to the exact same problem with the same qualitative conditions as in the laissez faire framework: (repeat) For a planned optimum at n^* it is necessary that the indifference curve must be a tangent to the factor-price frontier, and it is sufficient that the curvature of the indifference curve is algebraically larger than $\phi''(r^*)$.[56] Hence the sufficient condition (86), which we gave for the existence of a laissez faire optimum at n^*, is also valid for the planning framework. The only difference between the two maximization problems lies in the *degree* to which steady state utility differs from the social optimum/pessimum (we prove this in Appendix B).

---

[54] At this point, the comparison is solely between the laissez faire allocation and the two-part golden rule allocation which is chosen by the social planner (Samuelson (1968), p. 140). It is not possible to make other comparisons since some of the allocations aside from the laissez faire allocation and the two-part golden rule allocation, may not be feasible.

[55] The same can be found for the remaining two Cases 3 and 4 by combining the respective ends of Cases 1 and 2 as in Diagram 10 or 8.

[56] Once again reformulation of the condition (47) for n^* yields: $-k = \frac{-s}{(1+n^*)}$, which is nothing but the slope of the factor-price frontier equated to the slope of the indifference curve in the w, r space (Diamond (1965), p. 1140).

Hence, we have given a "more economic" reason why the problem of the optimum growth rate for population is "non-convex" (De La Croix and Michel (2002), p. 172). The argument given by De La Croix and Michel (2002), (p. 172) is that the Cobb-Douglas example by Deardorff (1976) shows that the problem is "non-convex". From the formal perspective it is now possible to state exact terms: the set of feasible allocations is defined by the convex factor-price frontier and is hence in general a concave set (Chiang and Wainwright (2005), p. 327). The factor-price frontier can be interpreted as a surrogate availability constraint.[57] Furthermore it appeared that the question of an optimum is closely related to the respective elasticities of substitution, but that these elasticities are not the exact criteria.

We can also conclude that the results derived by Michel and Pestieau (1993) remain valid for the laissez faire economy and hence that the Cobb-Douglas example of Deardorff (1976) is consistent with Case 2 with its counterintuitive change of efficiency at n^*. The same is obviously true for all CES cases with $\sigma > 1$ and $\tau > 1$.

After all we find that the reasoning of Samuelson (1975a) and Samuelson (1975b) remains fully valid as long as the economy behaves according to Case 1. However, the assertion of Samuelson (1975a), (p. 535) and Samuelson (1975b), (p. 542), which was never questioned by Deardorff (1976) or Michel and Pestieau (1993), that economies behave in general according to Case 1 is simply wrong.

[57] In principle it should also be possible to derive such a surrogate availability constraint for the c^1, c^2 plane, i.e. in Diagram 4, by varying the growth rate of population. However, the slope and curvature of such a curve involve complicated implicit expressions.

A different concept of Capital: The foregoing discussion of the optimum growth rate revealed that the best (worst) growth rate for population is always associated with the tangency of the (strictly convex, continuous and differentiable) factor-price frontier and the individual indifference curve. This means that a "Surrogate Production Function" was used, which implies an infinite number of technical blue-prints and a "jelly"-like concept of capital (Samuelson (1962), p. 201). We will now allow for more realism by assuming that there is only a finite number of technical blue-prints available.

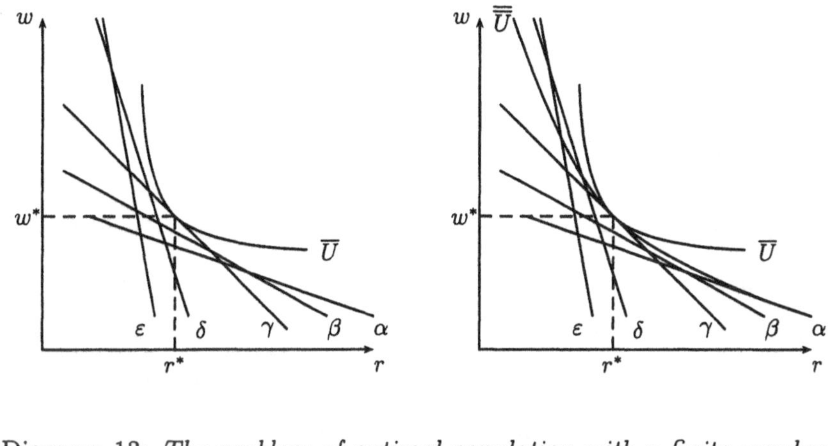

Diagram 13: *The problem of optimal population with a finite number of capital goods.*

Combining elements from Samuelson (1962), (p. 197) and Diamond (1965), (p. 1140)

The assumption of a finite number of technical blue-prints $\alpha, \beta, \gamma, \delta, \varepsilon$ changes the shape of the factor-price frontier, which remains continuous but is no longer strictly convex and differentiable. Diagram 13 reveals that once there are less than an infinite number of capital goods, the indifference curve can no longer be a tangent to the factor-price frontier from below (i.e. exhibit a smaller curvature).[58] Hence it is impossible that any growth rate for population, which is associated with the tangency of indifference curve and factor-price frontier, causes utility to fall to a minimum.

At this point we do not continue to formalize this argument concerning the number of different capital goods. The intention behind this diagrammatic discussion was only to show that it is the unrealistic assumption of an infinite number of capital goods which allows for a global or local minimum at some interior n^*.

2.4. Summary

Chapter 2, gave an overview over the discussion on the optimum growth rate for population in the neoclassical overlapping generations model of Diamond (1965). The key channels through which the growth rate of population influences the per capita steady state utility were isolated in the planning framework of the Solow (1956) growth model and the Samuelson (1958) consumption-loan model. The negative effect stemmed from the need to widen capital, the positive effect came from a permanent change in the age distribution of the population in favor of the young productive generation and thus cheaper old age consumption.

In the framework of the Diamond model both of these effects overlay each other. As discussed between Phelps (1967), Samuelson (1975a,

[58] This point is obviously by no means rigorous and does not hold for concave indifference curves (see Appendix B).

1975b, 1976), Deardorff (1976) and Michel and Pestieau (1993), it depends on the structure of the production and to a lesser extent on the consumption function whether these two effects overlay each other in a way that allows for an inner solution and a truly optimal growth rate of population. The crucial point[59] is, as Deardorff (1976) points out, whether it is assumed that an infinite capital intensity leads to infinite per capita output. In the special case of CES utility and production functions with elasticities of substitution smaller than one, there is an upper boundary for per capita output and utility. This is what allows for an interior maximum. Recent econometric estimates suggest that the respective elasticities of substitution lie, in the more important case of production only barely, below unity. In addition, Samuelson (1976) gives many good reasons why the elasticity should fall while the capital intensity runs toward infinity.

Another crucial result was the Serendipity Theorem which states that at the growth rate n^* the laissez faire equilibrium and the social optimum are compatible. This means that if there does exist only one unique stable steady state equilibrium, the economy automatically evolves into the social optimum optimorum provided that n was somehow set to the level n^*. If this steady state was a true optimum optimorum, there would be, from the normative point of view, no further need to explore the laissez faire behavior of the economy for $n \neq n^*$.

However, since it is not clear whether n^* really is the best or worst of all planned equilibria, the last section of this chapter was dedicated

[59]After our diagrammatic and formal discussion we consider different aspects as being more important.

to the question whether n^* would at least ensure that the economy ends up in the best of all laissez faire equilibria.

Treatment of this question revealed that it cannot be shown in general that the golden rule laissez faire equilibrium at n^* is the best among all laissez faire equilibria. Instead we found that the qualitative problem of optimum population growth in the laissez fair economy is identical with the planning problem. To treat the general problem of optimal population it is necessary to distinguish four different cases and only one of them (Case 1) was treated by Samuelson (1975a). The general sufficient condition for an interior optimum is given by $\frac{dr}{dn}_{|n=n^*} > 1$.

In the course of our diagrammatic discussion we revealed that it is the use of the "surrogate production function" of Samuelson (1962), which allows for a minimum at an intermediate growth rate for population, where the factor-price frontier is a tangent to the individual indifference curve. It is the unrealistic assumption of an infinite number of capital goods which allows for a global or local minimum at some interior n^*.[60]

Another interesting result was that an increase in the growth rate for population increases utility only when the economy experiences overaccumulation.

A positive result of this inquiry was that n^* is the only point were a change in the growth rate of population can trigger a change from a dynamically efficient (inefficient) steady state to one that is dynamically inefficient (efficient).

In my opinion, the results derived in the last section are a completion to the discussion of the optimum growth rate for population in the

[60]As previously noted, this argument does not hold for concave indifference curves.

Diamond (1965) model. It seems necessary and interesting to further explore the specific conditions which were posed concerning the existence of an optimum at n^*, which would make it necessary to further elaborate the second order derivative $U''(n)$.

Most important, however, is the question whether $\frac{dr}{dn}$ is larger or smaller than unity in a real world economy. Our own rough estimates for the $r - n$ relation, which are given in Appendix D, suggest that $\frac{dr}{dn}$ is in general much larger than unity.

3. Extensions to the Problem of the Optimum Growth Rate for Population in the Neoclassical Overlapping Generations Model

The intention in the previous chapter was to give a precise outline of the framework of analysis and the basic structure of the problem of optimal population growth. In this chapter, we will now introduce further aspects into the framework of analysis. These aspects will be:

1. Child-dependency costs:
   (a) Child-dependency costs as discussed by Arthur and McNicoll (1977) and Arthur and McNicoll (1978).
   (b) External effects induced by child-dependency costs and the validity of the Serendipity Theorem as discussed by Jaeger (1989).
2. Government debt.

The following aspects will be left out of consideration:

1. Endogenous fertility.
2. A savings behavior which is sensitive to the family size, i.e. $s = s(w, r, n)$.
3. Altruism, i.e. bequest and gift motives.
4. Endogenous technical progress.
5. Natural resources.

3.1. Child-dependency Costs

The previous discussion did not account explicitly for the fact that rearing children costs resources, instead Samuelson suggested: "As children they are part of their parents consumption and we take no note of them" (Samuelson (1958), p. 468). In this subsection we will take note of the fact that children cost resources like food, clothing, education and time of their parents. This means that there is now a second group of dependents. Each individual begins and ends its life as a dependent. This changes the situation fundamentally: In the two-period model an increase in the growth rate skewed the age distribution of society unambiguously in favor of the young productive ages. Now an increase in n has an ambiguous effect on the ratio of dependent and productive ages, since the demographic weight of children increases.

3.2. The Intergenerational Transfer Effect in a Model with Child-dependency Costs and Continuous Time

In this section we follow Arthur and McNicoll (1978) in reexamining the intergenerational transfer effect or, as Arthur and McNicoll (1978) call it, the "consumption-loan argument", which was discussed in Chapter 2. The discussion will basically amount to a restatement of the Arthur and McNicoll (1978) essay with a brief comment towards the end.

In a previous essay Arthur and McNicoll (1977) reexamined the entire optimization problem of Phelps (1967a) and Samuelson (1975a) in a model using integral-equation control theory. The main new assumption lies in the introduction of child dependency costs.[61] The qualitative results are basically the same as in Samuelson (1975a) and it still remains unclear whether there does exist an interior solution to the first order condition. And even if such a solution existed the sufficient conditions would have to be examined once again (Arthur and McNicoll (1977), p. 118).

Due to these complications Arthur and McNicoll (1978) took a different approach: Instead of going through the entire optimization problem, they try to focus only on the intergenerational transfer effect, which originates from changes in an arbitrarily given growth rate for population. Arthur and McNicoll (1978) argue that their continuous time "accounting framework" allows to measure the actual magnitude of the intergenerational transfer effect.

If it was possible to show that the transfer effect, which is not as robust as the capital widening effect (see the provisional result in the consumption-loan section of Chapter 2), is not positive for a real world economy with two groups of dependents, there would be only negative effects stemming from high population growth rates and thus population should decline as fast as possible. It would be unnecessary to check any sufficient conditions.

[61] Arthur and McNicoll (1977) also introduce a social time discount rate which leads to the typical modification of the first order conditions, i.e. the modified golden rule (Blanchard and Fischer (1989), p. 100). Another aspect is a "fertility control" parameter.

3.2.1. The Model

Instead of the two generations case, which was sufficient to study the general structure of the problem, Arthur and McNicoll (1978) use a more sophisticated model with continuous time. Individuals live for a continuous interval of time and there is an infinite number of generations which overlap each other. The advantage of such an accounting framework lies in its applicability to real world data and it can be used to calculate the actual magnitude of the transfer effect (Bommier and Lee (2003), p. 136).

The main new assumptions are:

1. Children impose costs, they have to be supported as dependents by the rest of society.

2. Children are treated as individuals from birth, with a welfare criterion that reflects their expected lifetime utility of consumption.

Further elements of the model are: net output is again distributed among consumption and investment:

$$F[K(t), L(t)] = C(t) + \dot{K}(t). \tag{88}$$

The growth rate of the stable population is given by n. At each point in time we have:[62]

$$B(t) \;=\; B(0)e^{nt}, \tag{89}$$

[62]In the following equations we will make use of the Riemann integral, which has an area as well as a sum connotation: $\int_a^b f(x)dx = \lim_{n\to\infty}\sum_{i=1}^{n} f(x_i)\Delta x_i = areaA$ (Chiang and Wainwright (2005), p. 457). We will also use the basic rules of integral calculus (Chiang and Wainwright (2005), Chapter 14) and the Leibnitz rule (Chiang (1992), p. 29).

$$\begin{aligned} L(t) &= \int_0^{\omega} B(t-x)p(x)\lambda(x)dx \\ &= B(t)\int_0^{\omega} e^{-nx}p(x)\lambda(x)dx, \end{aligned} \tag{90}$$

$$N(t) = \int_0^{\omega} B(t-x)p(x)dx = B(t)\int_0^{\omega} e^{-nx}p(x)dx. \tag{91}$$

Equation (89) gives the number of births at time t, (90) describes the labor supply $L(t)$ at each point in time, which depends on the maximum life span ω, the age dependent labor force participation of each generation $\lambda(x)$, and the probability of survival $p(x)$. The total population $N(t)$ is given by equation (91). Aggregate consumption is given by:

$$\begin{aligned} C(t) &= \int_0^{\omega} B(t-x)p(x)c(t,x)dx \\ &= B(t)\int_0^{\omega} e^{-nx}p(x)c(t,x)dx, \end{aligned} \tag{92}$$

where $c(t,x)$ is the per capita consumption of a representative individual aged x at time t. The labor-population ratio $\frac{L(t)}{N(t)}$ is denoted by h(n) and the birth rate $\frac{B(t)}{N(t)}$ by b(n). The average age of consuming is denoted by A_c, and the average age of the labor force is A_L with:

$$A_L := \frac{\int_0^{\omega} xe^{-nx}p(x)\lambda(x)dx}{\int_0^{\omega} e^{-nx}p(x)\lambda(x)dx}, \tag{93}$$

$$A_c := \frac{\int_0^{\omega} xe^{-nx}p(x)c(t,x)dx}{\int_0^{\omega} e^{-nx}p(x)c(t,x)dx}. \tag{94}$$

The availability constraint for the social planner is given by:

$$[f(k)-nk]\int_0^{\omega} e^{-nx}p(x)\lambda(x)dx = \int_0^{\omega} e^{-nx}p(x)c(x)dx. \tag{95}$$

Furthermore, Arthur and McNicoll (1978) assume that k is (somehow) adjusted so that the Phelps (1961) golden rule holds, i.e. per capita consumption is always maximized:

$$\frac{\partial \bar{c}}{\partial k} = f'(k) - n = 0; \qquad \bar{c} := \frac{C}{N}. \tag{96}$$

The Utility Function: According to the two assumptions made on the role played by children, each individual holds the following welfare function:

$$W = \int_0^{\omega} p(x) U[c(x)] dx. \tag{97}$$

Hence the problem of the social planner is to maximize per capita welfare subject to (95) and (96). This leads Arthur and McNicoll (1978), (p. 244), who choose not to derive this result, to the following first order condition, which implies the individual consumption behavior c(x):[63]

$$\frac{\partial U}{\partial c(0)} = e^{nx} \frac{\partial U}{\partial c(x)}. \tag{98}$$

Condition (98) is the biological interest rate relation of Samuelson (1958) for a model with continuous time.

[63]We do not go through the variational procedure to check this claim of Arthur and McNicoll (1978), especially since one of the constraints is an integral equation. However, it is not right away obvious that the probability of survival should be irrelevant, especially since the model of perpetual youth of Blanchard and Fischer (1989), (pp. 115-126) (especially pp. 121-122), clearly suggests that the probabilities of survival are of relevance for the consumption and accumulation behavior. This might also lead to a failure of the Serendipity Theorem.

3.2.2. The Welfare Implications of a Change in the Growth Rate of Population

This model can now be used to examine how a change in n influences steady state welfare of the representative individual by using (97) and (98). Differentiation of the welfare function with respect to n gives us:

$$\begin{aligned} dW &= \int_0^\omega p(x)\frac{\partial U}{\partial c(x)}\frac{\partial c(x)}{\partial n}dndx \\ &= \frac{\partial U}{\partial c(0)}\Big[\int_0^\omega e^{-nx}p(x)\frac{\partial c(x)}{\partial n}dx\Big]dn. \end{aligned} \tag{99}$$

Differentiation of the availability constraint (95) with respect to n and the use of (96) allows to rewrite (99):

$$\begin{aligned} &- [f(k)-nk]\int_0^\omega xe^{-nx}p(x)\lambda(x)dx - k\int_0^\omega e^{-nx}p(x)\lambda(x)dx \\ &= -\int_0^\omega xe^{-nx}p(x)c(x)dx + \int_0^\omega e^{-nx}p(x)\frac{\partial c(x)}{\partial n}dx. \end{aligned} \tag{100}$$

Inserting (the last term in) (100) into (99) gives:

$$\begin{aligned} dW &= \frac{\partial U}{\partial c(0)}\Big[\int_0^\omega \{-xe^{-nx}p(x)\lambda(x)[f(k)-nk] \\ &- ke^{nx}p(x)\lambda(x) + xe^{-nx}p(x)c(x)\}dx\Big]dn. \end{aligned} \tag{101}$$

Using (95), (93) and (94), we can rewrite (101) as:

$$\frac{dW}{dn} = \frac{\frac{\partial U}{\partial c(0)}}{b(n)}[\bar{c}(A_c - A_L) - kh(n)]. \tag{102}$$

Interpretation: Arthur and McNicoll (1978) interpret equation (102) as follows: $\frac{dW}{dn}$ is the steady state welfare effect, which consists of the ambiguous intergenerational transfer effect $\frac{\frac{\partial U}{\partial c(0)}}{b(n)}\bar{c}(A_c - A_L)$ and the negative capital widening effect $\frac{\frac{\partial U}{\partial c(0)}}{b(n)}(-kh(n))$.

The sign of the transfer effect depends on the difference between the production and the consumption pattern of the individuals, since the difference between income and consumption at each point in time has to be made up by transfers.

Using the representative schedules of labor participation, consumption and mortality, Arthur and McNicoll (1978) calculate $A_c = 36,6$ and $A_L = 39,8$ for developed countries. For less-developed countries they find $A_c = 29,4$ and $A_L = 33,9$. These values for A_c and A_L suggest that the transfer effect is in fact negative and that the optimum growth rate of population would be found at the lowest feasible level.

There are three objections which can be made:

1. The way in which A_c and A_L were calculated remains in the dark. Arthur and McNicoll (1978) do not explain how it is possible to use data from countries where, contrary to their assumption in (96), $r \neq n$ in order to calculate the transfer effect. Especially since the consumption behavior A_c might be changed according to the income and substitution effects, which occur when the government forces $r = n$ via an over- or under-funded pension system as in Samuelson (1975b). The same is true for A_L, which might also change if the government introduces over- or under-funded social security.
2. The assumption that children are treated as individuals from birth, i.e. that they are maximizing their lifetime utility by borrowing and lending, is obviously not realistic. In the next section, following Jaeger (1989), we will find that this unrealistic assumption is crucial to the problem of optimal population.
3. The accounting framework of Arthur and McNicoll (1978) has some things in common with the dependency approach of Jaeger (2002),

who shows that there always does exist an interior growth rate of population which minimizes the economic dependency burden, despite the fact that children cost resources.[64]

After all we can conclude that Arthur and McNicoll (1978) simply claim that once child dependency cost are included in the analysis the transfer effect turns out to be negative.

Concerning the framework of analysis we find that Arthur and McNicoll (1977) come up with similar first order conditions as Samuelson (1975a), and due to the continuous time framework, the problems with the sufficient conditions are even more severe. Bommier and Lee (2003) also conclude that their sophisticated continuous time framework reconfirms the results which were derived earlier in the simple discrete time models. Hence, we will now continue to use this technically less demanding approach.

3.3. The Serendipity Theorem and Child-dependency Costs

In this section we will follow Jaeger (1989), who reconsidered the validity of the Serendipity Theorem by introducing children as a second group of dependants into the framework of the Diamond model. One crucial

[64]It is obvious that the assumptions which constitute the dependency approach differ fundamentally from those of the neoclassical model and hence we can not say that the dependency approach can be used to prove Arthur and McNicoll (1978) wrong, but it gives at least a strong indication. The dependency approach of Jaeger (2002) will be outlined in Chapter 4.

difference, compared to the Diamond framework, lies in the use of a production function with fixed coefficients as in Harrod (1939).[65]

The Jaeger (1989) essay is divided into three main sections: the first section contains a discussion of the social optimum, the second section analyzes the laissez faire framework, and towards the end Jaeger introduces a social security system, which is necessary in the three generations case to bridge the gap between the social optimum and the market allocation.

3.3.1. The Model

Instead of a two-period life people now live for three periods. The crucial assumption is that children are not treated as individuals from birth. In their first period of life, each individual is supported by his parents through transfers, which means that the parents decide about the level of consumption of their children. In the second period, the individuals supply one unit of labor and receive their wages. In the third period, they live in retirement and consume principal and interest. The utility of each individual depends on the per capita consumption of his children and on his own consumption in the second and third period of life. Utility does not depend on the number of children.

The typical problem of stability which arises with a fixed-coefficient technology will be left out of consideration.

Utility: Utility is given by an ordinal utility function:

$$U(c^1, c^2, c^3); \tag{103}$$

[65]The conditions for the existence of a golden rule path in a Harrod-Domar model are given in Phelps (1967b), (pp. 15-17).

$$U_{c^i} > 0, \quad U_{c^ic^i} < 0, \quad U_{c^ic^j} \gtrless 0; \quad (i \neq j; \quad i,j = 1,2,3).$$

Where c^1 is the per capita consumption of children and c^2 and c^3 are the working age and retirement consumption.

Production: There is only one capital good and the fixed coefficient linear homogenous production function in the intensive form is given by:[66]

$$f(k) = Min[\lambda, \frac{k}{\bar{k}}]; \qquad \frac{1}{\bar{k}} > \delta > 0, \tag{104}$$

where $\bar{k}$ is the gross capital-output ratio and $\frac{1}{\lambda}$ is the technical labor-output ratio $\frac{L_{t-1}}{F}$. In this fixed-coefficient framework we will assume that the social planner controls the factor-prices.

3.3.2. The Social Optimum

The problem from the social planner's perspective is to maximize steady state utility subject to the availability constraint which is posed by the production function, the rate of deprecation, and the growth rate of population:

$$\begin{aligned} &\max \ _{c^1,c^2,c^3,n} U(c^1, c^2, c^3) \\ &\text{s.t.} \quad \lambda(1-(n+\delta)\bar{k}) = (1+n)c^1 + c^2 + \frac{c^3}{1+n}. \end{aligned} \tag{105}$$

Due to the fixed-coefficient technology, the capital intensity is no longer among the choice variables. The first order conditions to the maximization problem (105) are:

[66]Following Jaeger (1989) and Samuelson (1976) we do account for deprecation while we use the fixed-coefficient framework.

$$\frac{U_{c^1}}{U_{c^2}} = 1+n, \tag{106}$$

$$\frac{U_{c^2}}{U_{c^3}} = 1+n, \tag{107}$$

$$\frac{c^3}{(1+n)^2} = \lambda\bar{k} + c^1, \tag{108}$$

$$\lambda(1-(n+\delta)\bar{k}) = (1+n)c^1 + c^2 + \frac{c^3}{1+n}; \quad \frac{1}{\bar{k}} - \delta > n. \tag{109}$$

These conditions imply optimal values c^{1*}, c^{2*}, c^{3*} and n^*. Once again the sufficient conditions to these necessary conditions do not hold in general. In the case of a fixed coefficient production and consumption function it can be shown that for a high emphasis on old age consumption and a small capital intensity there does exist an $n^* > -\delta$ (Jaeger (1989), pp. 79-80).

3.3.3. The Laissez Faire Economy

The laissez faire behavior of the economy is characterized by the individual utility maximization problem:

$$\max_{c^1,c^2,c^3} U(c^1, c^2, c^3) \tag{110}$$

$$\text{s.t.} \quad \lambda(1-r\bar{k}) = (1+n)c^1 + c^2 + \frac{c^3}{1+r-\delta}.$$

With the following first order conditions:

$$\frac{U_{c^1}}{U_{c^2}} = (1+n), \tag{111}$$

$$\frac{U_{c^2}}{U_{c^3}} = (1+r-\delta), \tag{112}$$

$$\lambda(1-r\bar{k}) = (1+n)c^1 + c^2 + \frac{c^3}{(1+r-\delta)}. \tag{113}$$

Condition (111) shows that the individual allocation of resources between working age consumption and the consumption of children always satisfies the biological interest rate relation. Condition (112) shows that the individual allocation of resources between second period consumption and third period consumption depends on the market net real interest rate. Conditions (111)-(113) define the choice of the individual $\tilde{c^1}, \tilde{c^2}$ and $\tilde{c^3}$ for given values of r and n. However, in order to allow for a steady state equilibrium the life-cycle savings condition:

$$\frac{c^3}{(1+n)} = (1+r-\delta)\lambda\bar{k} \tag{114}$$

has to be met. Inspection of this condition reveals that c^3 is exogenously determined by (114), i.e. not determined through individual utility maximization as long as r and n are exogenously given. Hence the system (111)-(114) is over-determined.

3.3.4. A Second-Best Solution to the Problem of Optimal Population

The social planner can now improve this situation: In a first step it is possible to choose a factor-price $\tilde{r}$, which maximizes $U(\tilde{c^1}, \tilde{c^2}, \tilde{c^3})$ subject to (113) for a given growth rate n. The corresponding first order condition for the optimum gross interest rate $\tilde{r}$ is:

$$\frac{\tilde{c^3}}{(1+\tilde{r}-\delta)} = (1+\tilde{r}-\delta)\lambda\bar{k}. \tag{115}$$

In a second step, the social planner can vary the growth rate of population so that $n = \tilde{n} = \tilde{r} - \delta$.[67] By setting $n = \tilde{n} = \tilde{r} - \delta$, the

[67] It depends on the structure of the economy whether or not it is possible to set $n = \tilde{n} = \tilde{r} - \delta$; the conditions which have to be met to allow for such an intervention are given in Jaeger (1989), (p. 81).

central authority reaches the following second-best allocation: The life-cycle savings condition (114) does no longer differ from the first order condition (115), which defines the optimum factor-price $\tilde{r}$. Hence, conditions (111)-(113) and (115) (or (114)) now define an optimum with $\tilde{c^1}, \tilde{c^2}, \tilde{c^3}$ and $\tilde{r}$, where life-cycle savings are just sufficient to support this second-best steady state. This is the modified Serendipity Theorem of Jaeger (1989). Comparison of the first order conditions (106)-(109) for the social optimum with the conditions (111)-(113) and (115) for the second best allocation reveals that as long as we have $c^{1*}, \tilde{c^1} > 0$, we must have $\tilde{n} = \tilde{r} - \delta \neq n^*$.

3.3.5. Optimum Social Security

In a third step the central authority can improve the second-best allocation in order to ensure a utility level $U^* > \tilde{U}$ by introducing a fair $(n = r - \delta)$ social security system:

$$\alpha(1+n) = \beta, \tag{116}$$

with per capita contributions by the working age individuals of α and old age benefits of β. In the following, we will determine an optimal contribution α^* and use (116) to determine β. Once such a social security system is introduced, the life-cycle savings condition is altered:

$$\frac{c^3}{(1+n)} = (1+r-\delta)\lambda\bar{k} + \alpha; \quad n = r - \delta. \tag{117}$$

The new first order condition for the optimal $\tilde{r}$, which maximizes $\tilde{U}$ subject to the altered individual budget constraint[68], is now given by:

$$\frac{\tilde{c^3}}{(1+\tilde{r}-\delta)} = (1+\tilde{r}-\delta)\lambda\bar{k} + \alpha\frac{(1+n)}{(1+\tilde{r}-\delta)}. \tag{118}$$

[68] $\lambda(1-r\bar{k}) - (1+n)c^1 - c^2 - \frac{c^3}{(1+r-\delta)} + \alpha[\frac{(1+n)}{(1+r-\delta)} - 1] = 0.$

Once the social planner sets the level of contributions equal to the per capita costs of rearing children, we get:

$$\alpha^* = (1 + n^*)c^{1*}. \tag{119}$$

The conditions for a social optimum and the individual behavior, given α^*, are compatible (most notably (118), (117) and (108)), and for $\tilde{r} - \delta = r^* - \delta = n^*$ the optimal allocation with utility $U^* > \tilde{U}$ is reached. This means that once child dependency costs are repayed as contributions from the working age generation to their parents, which are the current retirees, through the social security system the optimum optimorum is reached. This implies that only in the special case where the working age generation makes voluntarily gifts to their parents, amounting to the *exact* rearing costs, the Serendipity Theorem would still be valid in this three generations case. In all other cases, where children repay only a fraction of their rearing costs, the optimum optimorum can only be reached through redistribution by the government through some sort of social security system.

Similar to the framework of Samuelson (1975a), changes in the growth rate of population have a negative capital widening effect on steady state utility and a positive effect since the retirees are supported by a larger working age population. The key difference in the three generations case lies in a third negative effect which stems from changes in the growth rate of population: A higher growth rate increases the number of children per working adult and thus it costs more resources to maintain a given level of per capita consumption c^1 of the children. This means that once the government tries to set n to the optimum level n^*, where the (marginal social) gains and losses resulting from the three effects are equal, the composition of the family consumption is altered and life-cycle savings do not just support the optimum optimorum. Only intervention via a social security system, which compensates the parents for their total rearing costs, allows to reach the social optimum where life-cycle savings are sufficient to just support the optimum optimorum (Jaeger (1989), pp. 86-87).

3.3.6. Provisional Result

Child-dependency costs are an obvious element to the problem of optimal population growth. There were two channels through which these costs alter the results obtained in the previous chapter:

1. The intergenerational transfer effect might turn out to be negative and population should decrease as fast as possible.

2. If the transfer effect remains positive despite the child-dependency costs, the Serendipity Theorem does not hold anymore as long as children are not treated as individuals from birth, except for the special case where children repay their *exact* rearing costs.

Related to this second point of Jaeger (1989) two things can be noted:

1. If children do not repay their exact rearing costs, the optimum optimorum can still be reached through government intervention via an optimal social security system.

2. If such an optimal social security system cannot be implemented, there may, depending on the structure of the economy, still exist an applicable second-best solution to the problem of optimal population.

At this point it seems that the perspective of an authority, which can control the growth rate of population, is stretched to its limits. If we continued from this point, it would now be necessary to complement the aspect of child-dependency costs by introducing endogenous fertility and the pleasures of parenthood. Nerlove et al. (1986), (p. 3), define endogenous fertility as follows: "By endogenous fertility ... we mean that parents determine the number of children they have and what they bequeath to them in form of physical or human capital in response to the economic constraints they face and in such a way as to maximize their own satisfaction". At this point the vast number of different approaches to endogenous fertility forbids to consider this intriguing matter.

3.4. Government Debt

Instead of allowing for some sort of endogenous fertility we will continue to treat the growth rate of population as an exogenous parameter. It is obvious that population is not exogenous but for the moment we cannot do any better and we thus continue to discuss how *given* changes in fertility affect steady state per capita utility. Once again, we will take no note of children. Children are included in their parents consumption as in Samuelson (1958).[69]

In the following section a government will be introduced into the framework of our two period overlapping generations model. The main

[69] Such an assumption, however, would suggest that the individual consumption pattern should also depend on the growth rate of population itself and not only on the changes in the factor-prices which originate from a change in the growth rate of population.

reference for the Diamond model with debt will be Diamond (1965) and De La Croix and Michel (2002), (pp. 179-237). The idea behind this approach is the following: Through-out this analysis the focus was on the allocation of resources. Since the government is a force that distorts the natural, i.e. market allocation of resources, the outcome of our previous analysis is sensitive to various government policies. The distortion of the market allocation can be beneficial once the government internalizes external effects (internal and external security, infrastructure, environmental issues and science), provided that the government failure does not exceed the market failure. The other kind of distortion comes into play when the government starts to distort market outcomes which are efficient. This second alternative seems to be widely neglected in the discussion concerning the optimum growth rate of population.

There is a wide variety of articles where the government solves inefficiencies via some sort of optimum social security or some other incentive to ensure optimum capital accumulation, or, in the case of endogenous fertility, it taxes or subsidizes parents in order to ensure optimal fertility. The main reason why the government is capable of pursuing such policies is that it is a participant with an infinite life expectancy. The government can use its intertemporal budget constraint to give the right incentives, which improve the market outcome generated by the short sighted individuals who live only for two periods.

In a democracy, however, things might be reversed since the typical administration lives only a very short life compared to the representative individual. So there are good reasons to assume that the government will rather use its intertemporal budget constraint to keep the current electorate happy at the expense of future generations (Persson and Tabellini (2000), pp. 117-132).[70] In the following, we will not account for this motive of the government explicitly, instead the only thing the government does is to run a constant per capita debt policy as in Diamond (1965). The basic question is whether or not a higher population growth rate might help to ease the individual burden posed by such a system.

We will proceed along the following lines: In a first step the Diamond (1965) model with internal government debt and the corresponding government budget constraint will be restated. In this framework we will concentrate on a government which runs a policy of constant internal debt. In a first step the social optimum will be examined. The second step is to derive the welfare implications of a change in the government debt policy, which leads us to the Diamond (1965) findings. The third step is to derive the welfare implications stemming from a change in the growth rate of population in a laissez faire economy with constant government debt.

3.4.1. The Model

The Diamond (1965) model with debt differs only with respect to the government budget constraint and the steady state life-cycle savings condition from the one introduced in Chapter 2. The net constant returns to scale production function is assumed to satisfy the Inada conditions

[70]The typical side-effects of debt and unfunded pay as you go social security systems like early retirement, excess burdens (the taxation needed to pay the interest), a lower capital intensity and lower wages, are usually overlooked (Feldstein (1974)). The strain felt by the individual in such a "social straitjacket" (Friedman (1999), p. 3) is also always neglected.

and is given by:

$$y = f(k); \quad f'(k) > 0; \quad f''(k) < 0.$$

Capital and labor are payed according to their marginal productivity. Individual utility is described by an ordinal utility function:

$$U = U(c^1, c^2),$$

which is characterized as in (2).

The Government Budget Constraint: Government debt yields the same interest as real capital and there is no risk of default. The debt has a one-period maturity. In each period the government has to finance the government expenditure G_t, it must service the matured debt B_{t-1}, and it has to pay interest amounting to $f'(k_t)B_{t-1}$. The government can use three tools to meet these obligations: it can raise a lump-sum tax $N_t\tau_t^1$ from the young generation, it can raise a lump-sum tax $N_{t-1}\tau_t^2$ from the old generation, or it can issue new debt B_t. Hence we have:

$$B_t + N_t\tau_t^1 + N_{t-1}\tau_t^2 = (1 + f'(k_t))B_{t-1} + G_t. \tag{120}$$

This budget constraint can be used for various intergenerational transfer policies with $B \gtreqqless 0$, $\tau^1 \gtreqqless 0$ and $\tau^2 \lesseqqgtr 0$. In the following, however, they will not be used as policy instruments. Instead, the government will simply pursue a constant per capita debt policy defined by:

$$\frac{B_{t-1}}{N_t} = b \quad \forall t. \tag{121}$$

The interest will be paid by issuing new debt and through a lump-sum tax on the young generation. In order to focus entirely on the welfare effects which originate from changes in the growth rate of population, government expenditure will be left out of consideration. Thus (120) simplifies to:

$$\tau^1 = [(1+f'(k_t)) - (1+n)]b = (f'(k_t) - n)b = \tau^1(k_t). \tag{122}$$

Equation (122) reveals that taxes can be either positive or negative depending on $b \gtrless 0$ and the sign of $(f'(k)-n)$, i.e. on whether the economy is in an efficient or inefficient state.

3.4.2. The Social Optimum

From the perspective of the social planner the problem remains unaltered. The availability constraint, which is not changed by such a debt policy, is given by:

$$f(k) - nk = c^1 + \frac{c^2}{(1+n)}, \tag{123}$$

and the problem of the social planner is:

$$\max_{c^2,k,n} U\Big(f(k) - nk - \frac{c^2}{(1+n)}, c^2\Big). \tag{124}$$

With the corresponding first order conditions:

$$\frac{U_{c^1}}{U_{c^2}} = 1+n, \tag{125}$$

$$f'(k) = n, \tag{126}$$

$$k = \frac{c^2}{(1+n)^2}. \tag{127}$$

Conditions (125)-(126) are the two-part golden rule, (127) is the condition for an optimum growth rate n^*. Together with the constraint (123), they define the optimal quantities c^{1*}, c^{2*}, k^* and n^*. These optimal values are identical to the ones which were derived for an economy without debt. The relevant tradeoff is still between capital widening and the intergenerational transfer effect.

3.4.3. The Competitive Economy with Government Debt

The individual utility maximization problem is given by:

$$\max_{c^1,c^2} \; U(c_t^1, c_{t+1}^2) \tag{128}$$
$$s.t. \quad w(k_t) - \tau_t^1(k_t) = c_t^1 + s_t; \quad c_{t+1}^2 = (1 + f'(k_{t+1}))s_t.$$

Thus the representative individual behaves according to:

$$\frac{U_{c^1}}{U_{c^2}} = 1 + f'(k_{t+1}), \tag{129}$$
$$s_t = w(k_t) - \tau_t^1(k_t) - c_t^1, \tag{130}$$
$$c_{t+1}^2 = (1 + f'(k_{t+1}))s_t. \tag{131}$$

3.4.4. Attainability of the Social Optimum

In a steady state equilibrium the life-cycle savings condition is given by:

$$s(w(k) - \tau^1(k), f'(k)) = (1+n)(b+k); \tag{132}$$
$$s = (1+n)(b+k) > 0,$$

where $s > 0$ is an obvious restriction since negative savings would lead to negative old age consumption. We can now compare the social optimum characterized by (123) and (125)-(127) with the conditions for the individual behavior by examining whether $(c^{1*}, c^{2*}, n^*, k^*)$ is a feasible laissez faire steady state equilibrium. Once we set $n = n^*$ and $k = k^*$, conditions (127) and (126) hold. According to (122) we have $\tau^1(k^*) = 0$ and the individual budget constraint[71] becomes the same as the availability constraint (123). In this case the individual will voluntarily choose c^{1*}

[71] That is: $f(k) - f'(k)k = c^1 + \frac{c^2}{(1+f'(k))} + \tau^1(k)$.

and c^{2*}. The last thing is to check the steady state life-cycle savings condition:

$$s^* = (1+n^*)k^* = \frac{c^{2*}}{(1+n^*)} \neq (1+n^*)(k^*+b); \quad \forall b \neq 0. \tag{133}$$

This means that since internal debt leads to the substitution of capital with debt (paper) in the portfolio of the representative individual,[72] the Serendipity Theorem does not hold.[73] Thus the only way to decentralize the social optimum is to reduce the per capita debt to zero.[74]

3.4.5. The Optimum Growth Rate for Population in a Competitive Economy

The comparison of the social optimum and the individual behavior revealed that the Serendipity Theorem does not hold in the Diamond model with internally held debt. Hence we will now assess the question of optimum population growth in a competitive economy. In the framework of De La Croix and Michel (2002), (pp. 216-230) it is possible to derive the impact on individual steady state utility resulting from:

1. A change in the constant debt policy for a given growth rate of population.[75]

[72] Diamond (1965), (p. 1141).

[73] Once the individuals face the biological rate of interest they voluntarily choose the optimal consumption patterns $c_n^2 = (1+n)s(w,r)$. However, some of the income saved goes into bonds instead of capital and hence, at a growth rate of n^*, capital formation (which was just sufficient to maintain k^* when *all* savings went into the formation of capital) falls short (for $b > 0$) of k^*.

[74] The Serendipity Theorem might still hold for external debt where there is no such substitution effect (Diamond (1965), p. 1137).

[75] This result will be useful once the first order conditions to the second question are derived.

2. A change in the growth rate of population for a given constant debt policy.

Temporary Equilibrium: There are several conditions which have to be met in each period to allow for a meaningful temporary equilibrium:

$$s_{t-1} > 0, \tag{134}$$

$$\tilde{w}(k_t, b) = w(k_t) - \tau^1(k_t) = w(k_t) - b(f'(k_t) - n) > 0, \tag{135}$$

$$s(\tilde{w}(k_t, b), f'(k_{t+1})) = (1+n)(k_{t+1} + b) > (1+n)b. \tag{136}$$

While (134) ensures positive consumption of the old generation, $\tilde{w}$ in (135) describes that the income after taxes of the current young individuals must be positive. Condition (136) must hold to allow for a positive capital intensity.

From (135) we can identify an upper bound $\bar{b}$ and a lower bound $\underline{b}$ for per capita debt.

Treatment of the upper and lower bounds for per capita debt allows to characterize a set of feasible temporary equilibria ε where the conditions (134)-(136) hold. Once such a set ε is established the life-cycle savings condition allows to identify the locus – in the k, b plane – of all steady state equilibria, which is a subset of ε. Instead of reproducing the sophisticated approach of De La Croix and Michel (2002), which after all leads to nothing new when compared to the Diamond (1965) essay (except for some rather dubious ideas on poverty traps (De La Croix and Michel (2002), p. 228)), we will use Diamond (1965) as the main reference from now on.

Steady State Equilibrium: In order to carry out the following comparative static (in per capita terms) analysis, it is necessary to determine the signs of $\frac{dk}{dn}$ and $\frac{dk}{db}$. Parallel to Chapter 2, we will have to use the correspondence principle in order to determine these signs. Hence the existence of a stable steady state equilibrium at some $\tilde{k} > 0$ will be assumed:[76]

$$0 < \frac{dk_{t+1}}{dk_t} = \frac{-s_{\tilde{w}}(\tilde{k}+b)f''(\tilde{k})}{(1+n) - s_r f''(\tilde{k})} < 1, \tag{137}$$

We will also assume that consumption in each period is a normal good:[77]

$$0 < s_{\tilde{w}} < 1. \tag{138}$$

Once debt is introduced into the model the new life-cycle savings condition has to reflect that the individuals have to accumulate capital and buy the newly issued government debt in pace with population growth:

$$s(\tilde{w}(k,b), f'(k)) = (1+n)(k+b). \tag{139}$$

Total differentiation of (139) with $db = 0$ leads to:

$$\frac{dk}{dn}_{|db=0} = \frac{k + (1 - s_{\tilde{w}})b}{s_r f'' - (1+n) - s_{\tilde{w}}(k+b)f''} < 0. \tag{140}$$

The sign in the denominator of the expression (140) is negative by virtue of the stability condition (137). Due to assumption (138) and conditions (134) and (136) the sign of the numerator is positive. Total differentiation of (139) with $dn = 0$ yields:

$$\frac{dk}{db}_{|dn=0} = \frac{(1+n) + s_{\tilde{w}}(f' - n)}{s_r f'' - (1+n) - s_{\tilde{w}}(k+b)f''} < 0. \tag{141}$$

---

[76]Contrary to Diamond (1965), we will conduct the comparative static analysis (in per capita terms) rather in terms of the capital intensity than the real interest rate. The stability condition (137) can be obtained from (136).

[77]Diamond (1965), (pp. 1131-1134).

Assumption (138) reveals that the sign in the numerator of (141) must be positive. The sign of the denominator is negative according to (137).

Once the signs of $\frac{dk}{dn}$ and $\frac{dk}{db}$ are known to be negative the key elements to our question can be displayed in Diagram 14.

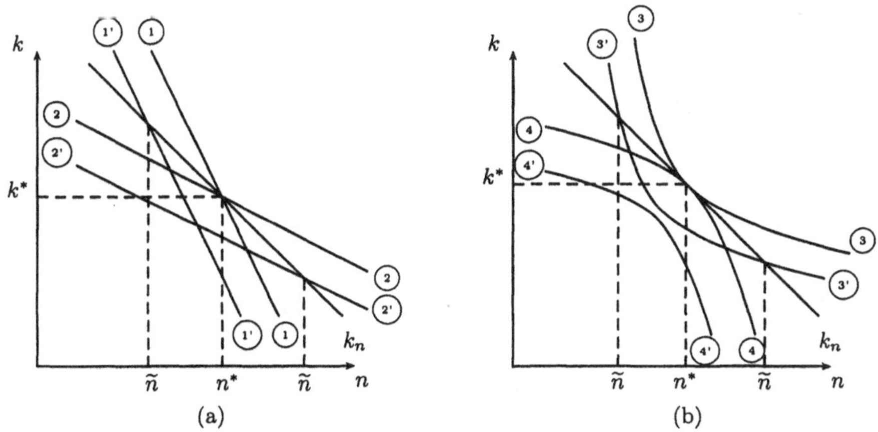

Diagram 14: *Golden rule growth and debt.*

Diagram 14 (a) and (b) display the four different possible loci of the laissez faire steady state equilibria which were discussed in the laissez faire framework of Chapter 2. The k_n line gives the respective golden rule capital intensities and separates the efficient from the inefficient equilibria. Once the government issues debt (the debt loci have an apostrophe) these loci shift according to $\frac{dk}{db} < 0$ and the growth rate of population which leads to a golden rule allocation changes from n^* to $\tilde{n}$.

3.4.6. Debt and Welfare

After these preparations the Diamond (1965) result concerning the welfare implications of a change in the constant per capita internal debt policy can be reproduced: From the life-cycle savings condition (132) and the respective factor-prices one obtains the following indirect utility function:[78]

$$U(c^1, c^2) =$$
$$U\Big(f(k) - kf'(k) - (1+n)(k+b) - \tau^1(k), (1+f')(1+n)(k+b)\Big). \quad (142)$$

Using (122) allows to rewrite (142):

$$U(c^1, c^2) =$$
$$U\Big(f(k) - kf'(k) - (1+n)k - (1+f'(k))b, (1+f'(k))(1+n)(k+b)\Big).$$

The first order derivative of per capita utility with respect to the debt level is:

$$\begin{aligned} \frac{dU}{db} &= -U_{c^1}\Big([f''(k+b) + (1+n)]\frac{dk}{db} + (1+f')\Big) \\ &+ U_{c^2}\Big(f''(1+n)(k+b) + (1+f')(1+n)\Big)\frac{dk}{db} \\ &+ U_{c^2}(1+f')(1+n). \end{aligned} \quad (143)$$

Condition (129), which describes the individual consumption pattern, allows to reformulate (143):

$$\frac{dU}{db} = U_{c^1}(n-f')\Big(1 + \frac{(k+b)}{(1+f')}f''\frac{dk}{db}\Big) \gtreqless 0. \quad (144)$$

Equation (144) reveals that the sign of $\frac{dU}{dn}$ depends solely on the sign of $(n-f')$, since we know from the stability condition (137) that $\frac{dk}{db} < 0$.

[78] For the steady state capital intensity we have $k = k(n, b)$ with $\frac{dk}{db} < 0$ and $\frac{dk}{dn} < 0$.

Hence an increase of per capita debt increases (decreases) per capita utility if the economy is experiencing over-accumulation (under-accumulation) in the steady state equilibrium (Diamond (1965), pp. 1142-1143).

3.4.7. Population and Welfare

After these preparations the welfare implications, which originate from a change in the growth rate of population, can be derived. The utility function is again given by:

$$U(c^1, c^2) =$$
$$U\Big(f(k) - kf'(k) - (1+n)k - (1+f'(k))b, (1+f'(k))(1+n)(k+b)\Big).$$

The first derivative with respect to the growth rate of population is:

$$\begin{aligned}\frac{dU}{dn} &= -U_{c^1}\Big([(k+b)f'' + (1+n)]\frac{dk}{dn} + k\Big) \\ &+ U_{c^2}\Big((1+n)(1+f') + f''(1+n)(b+k)\Big)\frac{dk}{dn} \\ &+ U_{c^2}(1+f')(k+b). \end{aligned} \tag{145}$$

Using (129), we obtain:

$$\frac{dU}{dn} = U_{c^1}b + U_{c^1}\frac{(n-f')(k+b)}{1+f'}f''\frac{dk}{dn} \gtreqless 0. \tag{146}$$

From the stability condition (137) we have $\frac{dk}{dn} < 0$ and consequently equation (146) indicates the following: At the growth rate of population $\tilde{n}(\neq n^*)$, where the laissez faire economy satisfies the two-part golden rule, i.e. $f'(k(\tilde{n}, b)) = \tilde{n}$, the sign of $\frac{dU}{dn}$ in (146) depends solely on $b \gtrless 0$. This allows the following conclusion:

Theorem 3: *In a laissez faire economy with constant per capita government debt/pay-as-you-go social security the growth rate of population, which leads to a golden rule allocation, can never be optimal.*

The first order derivative (146) contains two elements: The first element $U_{c^1}b > 0$ (for $b > 0$) is the biological interest rate effect, which suggests that population should grow as fast as possible (compare with (7)).[79] The reason for the appearance of the biological interest argument is the following: Each young individual buys government debt amounting to $(1+n)b$ and pays taxes $(f'(k)-n)b$. Hence the young individual hands over a total amount of $(1+f'(k))b$ to the government. In the retirement period, the government serves its obligations and pays $(1+f'(k))(1+n)b$. Hence the individual receives the biological rate of interest $(1+n)$ on its total payments. This also reveals that the total amount of resources which is transferred into the retirement period, at the biological rate of interest, depends on the rate of interest $(1+f'(k))$ and hence, via the capital intensity, on the growth rate of population.

The second element $U_{c^1}\frac{(n-f')(k+b)}{1+f'}f''\frac{dk}{dn}$ describes the factor-price effects which originate from a change in the growth rate of population. An increase in n leads to a fall in k, which increases the interest rate payed on capital and bonds, and decreases wages.

In the special case $b = 0$, (146) degenerates into (81) where $\frac{dU}{dn} = 0$ for $n = n^*$, and at n^* the pair of factor-prices $w(k(n^*)), r(k(n^*))$ ensure maximum (minimum) lifetime utility. The tradeoff is solely between wages and interest.

[79] From the formal perspective we have: $\frac{\partial U}{\partial n} = -U_{c^1}k + U_{c^2}(1+f'(k))(k+b) = U_{c^1}b$.

In the case $b \neq 0$ the situation differs fundamentally: as (146) indicates, the tradeoff is now between what we will call the aggregate factor-price effects and the biological interest rate. This altered situation stems from the government debt policy. The growth rate which maximizes (minimizes) laissez faire utility in an economy with government debt will be referred to as n^{**}.

As discussed in Chapter 2 it depends on the structure of the economy whether there does exist an optimum growth rate of population or not. A diagrammatic exposure of the Cases 1 and 2 with government debt is given in Diagram 15:

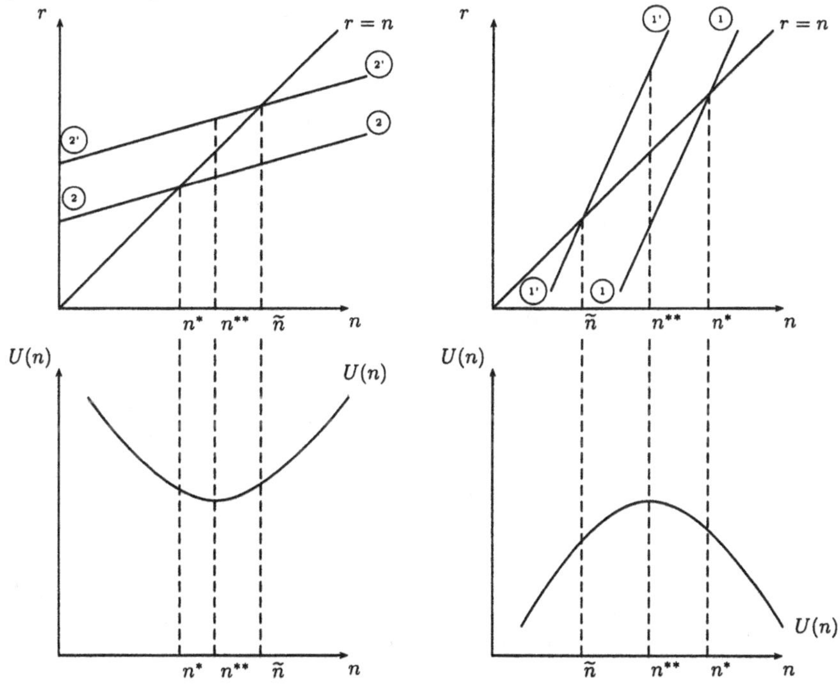

Diagram 15: *The optimum/pessimum growth rate for population n^{**} with government debt.*

Using Case 1 as the example, the discussion concerning the optimum growth rate of population can be summarized in the familiar four quadrant diagram:

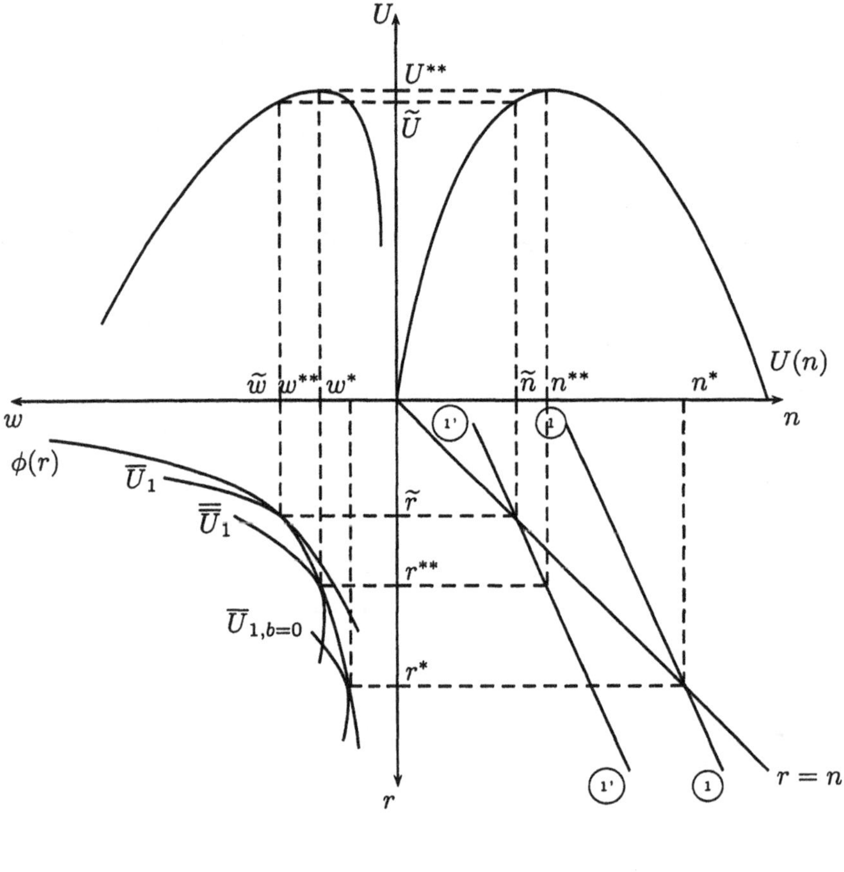

Diagram 16: *The problem of optimal population in the neoclassical overlapping generations model with government debt.*

Diagram 16 illustrates that the optimum growth rate of population n^{**} differs from the optimum growth rate of population in the case without debt. The preference ordering is changed by the introduction of debt, since the interest rate is not only determining the relative price of future and current consumption. The interest rate also determines the total amount of resources which go through the hands of the government and yield the biological interest rate. Thus the indifference curves with debt $\bar{U}_1$ and $\bar{\bar{U}}_1$ may intersect the indifference curve $\bar{U}_{1,b=0}$. At the optimum growth rate of population n^{**} we have $(n - f') < 0$. Hence the government can always improve steady state utility through a reduction of per capita debt. The (social) optimum optimorum would once again be reached at n^* with $b = 0$. Since the idea behind this inquiry was that high growth rates might increase the utility of the representative individual, we can note that n^{**} is larger than the growth rate $\tilde{n}$ which causes a golden rule allocation, and it may or may not be larger than n^*. The conditions which have to be met to allow for a laissez faire (planned) optimum at n^{**} (n^*) remain basically unaltered with $\frac{dr}{dn} > 1$; the only difference is that in the case with debt the difference $(n - f'(k(n)))$ must increase sufficiently to allow for an interior optimum at n^{**}.

The claim that Theorem 3 and the other qualitative results for an economy with government debt remain also valid in an economy with pay-as-you-go social security is substantiated in Appendix F.

3.4.8. Provisional Result

In Chapter 2 we treated a) the planned economy and b) a laissez fair economy. In Chapter 3 we discussed c) a laissez faire economy with government debt. The respective tradeoffs associated with the growth rate of population were:

a) In the planning framework the relevant tradeoff was between capital widening and the intergenerational transfer effect.

b) In a laissez faire economy without social security and debt the tradeoff is between wages and interest.

c) In an economy with an unfunded social security system and/or debt the tradeoff is between the aggregate factor-price effects and the intergenerational transfer effect.

The results from the foregoing section can be summarized as follows:

1. The allocation, which describes the optimum optimorum in the planned economy is unaffected by a constant debt policy, but the Serendipity Theorem does not hold anymore.

2. For a given growth rate of population, the classical Diamond (1965) result suggests that issuing debt raises per capita utility only in an economy which experiences over accumulation. In such an economy debt should be issued up to the point where golden rule growth is attained.

3. For a given debt policy ($b > 0$) the growth rate for population should be set to a level where the marginal productivity of capital exceeds the growth rate for population and, contrary to all previous results, not to the level where golden rule growth is attained.

3.5. Summary

In this chapter we allowed for more realism by introducing child-dependency costs and government debt into the overlapping generations model discussed in Chapter 2.

Once child dependency costs were introduced we had a second group of dependants in the economy. This led Arthur and McNicoll (1978) to the conclusion that the intergenerational transfer effect would, due to the additional burden of rearing children, turn negative and that the population should decrease as fast as possible. One critical assumption in this framework was that children were treated as individuals from birth.

Without the assumption that children maximize their utility as independent individuals from birth, Jaeger (1989) showed that the Serendipity Theorem does not hold anymore.

Therefore, the conclusion was that there might not exist an interior optimum growth rate of population and if it existed, the Serendipity Theorem does not hold. A social security system has to be put in place in order to ensure that the economy reaches the optimum optimorum.

The second part of this chapter was concerned with government debt. The optimum growth rate of population in a laissez faire economy with constant per capita debt was discussed. The main references for the framework of analysis were Diamond (1965) and De La Croix and Michel (2002).

The results were the following: government debt does not change the optimal quantities c^{1*}, c^{2*}, k^*, n^* of the social optimum. Due to the substitution of capital and debt (paper) in the portfolios of the representative individuals the Serendipity Theorem does not hold anymore. However, once the Serendipity Theorem does not hold there is still another growth rate of population $\tilde{n}(\neq n^*)$ where the laissez faire economy evolves into a steady state which satisfies the two-part golden rule. According to the first order conditions for the optimum growth rate of population in a laissez faire economy, this golden rule steady state can never be optimal. Instead the optimum (pessimum) occurs at a growth rate n^{**} with $n^{**} \lesseqqgtr n^*$ and $n^{**} \neq \tilde{n}$.

The tradeoff, which is relevant on the individual level, is not between wages and interest as in the laissez faire economy discussed in Chapter 2. It is also not between the capital widening effect and the intergenerational transfer effect. Instead, the relevant tradeoff is now between the aggregate factor-price effects and the biological interest rate, which the individual receives (after taxes) from holding debt. In such a situation the relevance of the biological interest rate relations of Samuelson (1958) and Phelps (1961) as *the* objective ceases. For the most plausible case, i.e. Case 1, the optimum growth rate of population n^{**} is larger than $\tilde{n}$ and we have $f'(k(n^{**})) > n^{**}$.

4. The Optimum Growth Rate for Population Derived from the Economic Dependency Ratio

In the foregoing two chapters the question of an optimum growth rate for population was discussed in the framework of the basic one-sector neoclassical growth model and the neoclassical overlapping generations model. The criterion was individual steady state utility. In Chapter 2 the basic structure and the decisive points and problems were elaborated. In Chapter 3 some of the problems from Chapter 2 were revisited by introducing further aspects into the framework of analysis.

In this chapter we leave the neoclassical growth model with its endogenously determined per capita income, factor-prices and utility maximizing individuals. Instead, we will now turn to an alternative criterion for the optimum growth rate of population: the economic dependency ratio. There are various different frameworks which allow to use the dependency ratio, given in: Jaeger (2002), Weil (1999), Schmitt-Rink (1989) and Rodriguez (1988). In the following, we will outline only the central idea behind the dependency approach.

The reason to introduce this approach is the following: in Chapters 2 and 3 it became obvious that the neoclassical model is a very rich economic model, but when it comes to determining an actual optimum growth rate for population, the answer is that the magnitude of n^* or n^{**} depends on the structure of the economy. Especially on the respective elasticities of substitution, which can only be estimated roughly. In addition, as Samuelson (1976) points out, once the growth rate of population changes, the capital intensity also changes and with the capital intensity the elasticity of substitution between capital and labor. This means that even if the current estimates of σ and τ were correct, they might still be misleading once n and k are changed.

For the dependency approach we find the opposite: the dependency approach is rather weak when it comes to explaining the economic behavior of an economy over time. On the other hand, the dependency ratio is very strong when it is necessary to actually determine an optimum growth rate for population. Hence, the dependency approach appears to be closing a gap which became more and more apparent in the previous two chapters.

In a first step we will introduce this alternative approach, using Jaeger (2002) as the main reference. The second part will briefly pick up on some further aspects, which are often referred to in the literature dealing with the dependency approach. The main references will be Weil (1999) and Jaeger (2002).

4.1. The Dependency Approach

The economic dependency ratio differs fundamentally from our previous criteria. In the different types of the neoclassical model the per capita total *amount* of physical units of output available for consumption, or per capita utility were used as criteria to identify an optimal growth rate for population. The dependency ratio is a different criterion, which is focused on *shares* instead. Hence, the optimum growth rate which minimizes the economic dependency burden will be denoted by n^{***}.

4.1.1. The Model

The following simple model will capture the essence of the dependency approach and allows to calculate an actual n^{***}. In this model there are four generations alive, at each point in time t the total population is consisting of:

1. N_t dependent children aged 0-19 years.
2. N_{t-1} members of the young and active generation aged 20-39 years.
3. N_{t-2} the old active generation aged 40-59 years.
4. N_{t-3} the dependent retired generation aged 60-79 years.

The probability that a child reaches the age $20-39$ is given by α, the probability that a young adult reaches the age $40-59$ is β and the probability that an old adult reaches the age $60-79$ is given by γ. There is no aggregate uncertainty and individuals die at the end of their retirement period with certainty. Only the young productive generation has children; hence we have:

$$N_t = (1+n)\alpha N_{t-1}, \tag{147}$$

and

$$\begin{aligned} N_{t-1} &= \frac{N_t}{\alpha(1+n)}; \quad N_{t-2} = \frac{N_{t-1}}{\alpha(1+n)} = \frac{N_t}{\alpha^2(1+n)^2}; \\ N_{t-3} &= \frac{N_t}{\alpha^3(1+n)^3}. \end{aligned} \tag{148}$$

Using the survival probabilities, the number of people in their working age $(20-59)$ can be expressed as:

$$\alpha N_{t-1} + \alpha\beta N_{t-2} = \frac{N_t}{(1+n)} + \frac{\beta N_t}{\alpha(1+n)^2}. \tag{149}$$

Equations (148) and (149) allow to define the demographic ratio R_1 between children and adults in their working age:

$$R_1 := \frac{\alpha(1+n)^2}{\alpha(1+n)+\beta}, \tag{150}$$

and the demographic ratio R_2 between retirees and working age population:

$$R_2 := \frac{\beta\gamma}{\alpha^2(1+n)^2+\alpha\beta(1+n)}. \tag{151}$$

Hence the demographic ratio R between dependents and working age population is:

$$R := R_1 + R_2. \tag{152}$$

This demographic dependency ratio can now be transformed into an economic dependency ratio by attaching economic weights u_1 and u_2 to the respective dependents. The parameter u_i, $(i = 1, 2)$ gives the percentage of income of a working individual which must be used to support a child/retired dependent. In the following, we assume that u is a given parameter which does not depend on the growth rate of population. Thus the economic dependency ratio Q can be defined as:

$$\begin{aligned} Q : &= v_1 + v_2 = u_1 R_1 + u_2 R_2 \\ &= u_1 \frac{\alpha(1+n)^2}{\alpha(1+n)+\beta} + u_2 \frac{\beta\gamma}{\alpha^2(1+n)^2+\alpha\beta(1+n)}. \end{aligned} \tag{153}$$

Equation (153) describes the percentage of income Q, which the average working individual has to give up to support the dependents; v_1 goes to the children, v_2 to the retirees. Before we give the first order condition for an optimum growth rate, we note the following properties of $Q(n)$: for v_1 and v_2 we find $\frac{dv_1}{dn} = u_1 \frac{\alpha^2(1+n)^2+2\alpha\beta(1+n)}{(\alpha(1+n)+\beta)^2} > 0$ and

$\frac{dv_2}{dn} = u_2 \frac{-\alpha\beta\gamma(2\alpha(1+n)+\beta)}{(\alpha^2(1+n)^2+\alpha\beta(1+n))^2} < 0$. Concerning the limit of $Q(n)$ one finds $Q(n) \to \infty$ for $n \to \infty$ and $n \to -1$. Thus Q is strictly convex in n and hence there does exist an intermediate growth rate n^{***} which minimizes Q (Jaeger (2002), p. 278).

The first order condition for the optimum growth rate of population is:

$$\begin{aligned} \frac{dQ}{dn} &= \frac{dv_1}{dn} + \frac{dv_2}{dn} \\ &= u_1 \frac{\alpha^2(1+n)^2 + 2\alpha\beta(1+n)}{(\alpha(1+n)+\beta)^2} - u_2 \frac{\alpha\beta\gamma(2\alpha(1+n)+\beta)}{(\alpha^2(1+n)^2+\alpha\beta(1+n))^2} \\ &= 0. \end{aligned} \tag{154}$$

Using the binomial formulas, condition (154) can be simplified:[80]

$$\begin{aligned} \frac{dQ}{dn} &\gtreqless 0 \\ \Leftrightarrow u_1\alpha^3(1+n)^3[\alpha(1+n)+2\beta] &\gtreqless u_2\alpha\beta\gamma[2\alpha(1+n)+\beta]. \end{aligned} \tag{155}$$

From (155) we can now obtain the sign of $\frac{dQ}{dn}$ for a stationary population ($N_t = N_{t-1}$) where $\alpha(1+n^0) = 1$ holds. This sign indicates whether the optimum growth rate n^{***} is positive or negative:

$$\frac{dQ}{dn}_{|n^0} \gtreqless 0 \quad \Leftrightarrow \quad u_1(1+2\beta) \gtreqless u_2\alpha\beta\gamma(2+\beta). \tag{156}$$

Depending on the respective probabilities of survival α, β, γ, and the economic weights u_1 and u_2, the sign of $\frac{dQ}{dn}$ varies.

Given the mortality schedule ($\alpha = 0,995; \beta = 0,9705; \gamma = 0,47575$), different ratios $\frac{u_2}{u_1}$ lead to the following optimum growth rates for Germany:

[80]The first step is to rearrange (154) so that we have: $u_1 \frac{\alpha^2(1+n)^2+2\alpha\beta(1+n)}{(\alpha(1+n)+\beta)^2} = u_2 \frac{\alpha\beta\gamma(2\alpha(1+n)+\beta)}{(\alpha^2(1+n)^2+\alpha\beta(1+n))^2}$ multiplying with $(\alpha^2(1+n)^2 + \alpha\beta(1+n))^2$ and rearranging gives: $u_1 \frac{\alpha^4(1+n)^4(\alpha^2(1+n)^2+2\alpha\beta(1+n)+\beta^2)+2\alpha^3\beta(1+n)^3(\alpha^2(1+n)^2+2\alpha\beta(1+n)+\beta^2)}{(\alpha(1+n)+\beta)^2} = u_2\alpha\beta\gamma(2\alpha(1+n)+\beta)$. Now the binomial formulas and rearrangement allow to obtain (155).

Table 3: **Optimal growth rates for Germany**

$\frac{u_2}{u_1}$	2,237	2,0	1,8	1,673
n^{***} in percent p.a.	0,0774	-0,147	-0,3547	-0,5284

Source: Jaeger (2002), (p. 281)

These numbers are in line with the findings in the literature using the economic dependency ratios as the criterion for n^{***}. Typically the growth rates for developed countries are slightly negative and they depend positively on the ratio $\frac{u_2}{u_1}$. This means that if the old ages are very expensive (cheap) to support compared to the young ages, the age distribution should be skewed more (less) in favor of the young ages.

If there were no rearing costs for children, i.e. $u_1 = 0$, there would be no interior solution and the fastest feasible growth rate would be the best. We would have the same result as in the consumption-loan model of Chapter 2.

4.1.2. Further Aspects

The foregoing section outlined the key idea of the dependency approach. There is another aspect which can be treated in such a framework: The large changes in the economic dependency ratio during the period of transition from one stable population to another. The main argument is:[81] the transition towards slower population growth always leads to

[81] At this point we will refer to Weil (1999) and the dependency approach. It is however clear that Weil (1999) is not the first one to come up with these points. It is

relatively large decreases in the economic dependency burden, since the number of children decreases immediately, but it takes considerable time till the weight of the old generation increases. The opposite is true for an increase in the growth rate of population where costs increase right away due to a greater number of children, but the favorable effect of a lower weight of the retirees is delayed. Weil (1999), (pp. 252-254) gives a diagrammatic discussion of this point portraying various fertility scenarios for the United States.

The argument that there is a favorable effect stemming from the reduction of fertility brings up one point: regardless of whether the criterion is a dependency ratio or per capita utility, the question of an optimum growth rate for population with a stable age distribution is a very artificial one. The question might instead well be: what is the optimal time path for the growth rate itself. The respective criterion might be served much better by continuous reductions of n, below n^* or n^{**} or n^{***}, so that a steady state as discussed in Chapters 2 and 3 might be completely insignificant.

On the other hand, onc can also take a different stance concerning these favorable effects of lowering the growth rate of population. Drucker (1997), (p. 20) comments: "The developed world is in the process of committing collective suicide. Its citizens are not having enough babies to reproduce themselves, and the cause is quiet clear: its younger people are no longer able to bear the increasing burden of older, non-working people". There might be numerous people who do not enjoy a

also clear that the transition from one stable population to another can also be studied in the neoclassical framework (Jaeger (1972)).

low dependency burden which is associated with the extinction of their nation. In addition, the representative individual might be very sensitive towards the composition of the group of dependents. A shrinking population implies that some of the dependents are not members of the respective families and people might dislike to pay for the retirement of strangers.

Another point is that the growth rate n^{***} is much easier to estimate than n^{*} and it should be interesting to examine how these growth rates are exactly related. Such a relation between golden rule growth and the dependency approach is loosely given in Jaeger (2002), (pp. 285-286), and Schmitt-Rink (1989), (pp. 52-62).

4.1.3. Summary

The economic dependency criterion is a straightforward approach to identify an optimum growth rate for population. Compared to the neoclassical growth model there are two main advantages:

1. Contrary to the indirect utility function, which was not strictly concave in n, the dependency ratio Q is convex in n, which ensures an inner minimum and hence the existence of an optimal n^{***}.

2. There are less data required to calculate an actual n^{***} and the data are different. In the neoclassical framework as discussed in Chapter 2 it is necessary to know the structure of the whole economy, i.e. the utility and production function, which can only be roughly estimated. In contrast, the dependency approach requires only data which are provided by national statistic bureaus, and

the methods of estimation (mortality schedules and the costs of retirees/children) are probably more reliable.

On the other hand there is one severe shortcoming of the dependency approach, which lies in the fact that the optimum growth rate n^{***}, except for some special cases of coincidence, cannot be expected to be equal to n^{*} or n^{**}. Thus n^{***} minimizes the economic dependency ratio, i.e. the share of per capita income that goes to the dependents, but it does not maximize lifetime well-being.

5. Conclusion

Our theoretical starting point was the pure consumption-loan model of Samuelson (1958). This overlapping generations framework with exogenous per capita income allows to isolate two relevant aspects to the question of optimal population growth in the neoclassical overlapping generations model:

1. Every increase in the growth rate of population has a positive effect: it skews the age distribution of a stable population permanently in favor of the young productive ages. There are more workers to support each retiree.

2. Given the growth rate of population, maximum steady state utility is attained when the interest rate on consumption-loans equals the growth rate of population. This biological interest rate relation, for the consumption pattern, was a landmark, which reappeared throughout the entire discussion of the problem of optimal population in the neoclassical overlapping generations model.

In a second step we used the neoclassical one-sector growth model following Solow (1956) with its emphasis on capital accumulation and the production function. This framework allowed to isolate two further aspects:

1. Every increase in the growth rate of population has a negative effect; it increases the need to "waste" resources on capital widening.

2. For a given growth rate of population, capital should be accumulated up to the point where the net real interest rate of capital

equals the growth rate of population. Such an accumulation pattern maximizes steady state per capita consumption. It is the second crucial biological interest rate relation.

After these preparations, we followed the discussion surrounding the Phelps (1967a) and Samuelson (1975a) attempt to derive an interior optimum growth rate for population in the Diamond (1965) model without government debt. The key points were:

1. The Diamond (1965) model is a blend of both: the pure consumption-loan model and the neoclassical one-sector growth model. The positive intergenerational transfer effect and the negative capital widening effect come both into play and allow for an intermediate optimum growth rate for population.

2. Together, the two biological interest rate relations form the two-part golden rule, which describes a true (local) social optimum for every arbitrarily given growth rate of population.

3. Among all optimal steady states which satisfy the two-part golden rule, the optimum optimorum can be reached by setting the growth rate of population to its optimal level n^*. Deardorff (1976) and Michel and Pestieau (1993) show that the existence of an optimum growth rate n^* depends on the elasticity of substitution between capital and labor, and to a lesser extent on the elasticity of intertemporal substitution between young and old age consumption. If both elasticities are positive and below unity, as suggested by recent econometric analysis, there does exist an interior optimum optimorum.

4. Once the growth rate of population is set to the optimal level, the Serendipity Theorem of Samuelson (1975a) is valid: "At the optimum growth rate n^*, private lifetime savings will just support the most golden golden rule lifetime state".

5. Our reconsideration of the optimum growth rate of Samuelson (1975a) in a laissez faire framework revealed that $\frac{dr}{dn} > 1$ is the *exact* sufficient condition for a laissez faire optimum at n^*. In a second step, we found that the conditions for a planned optimum at n^* are identical to those in the laissez faire framework. Our own estimates suggest that $\frac{dr}{dn}$ is larger than unity for a real world economy.

6. In a laissez faire economy, increases in the growth rate of population only increase steady state utility if the economy is growing on a dynamically inefficient path.

7. It is the use of the "surrogate production function" of Samuelson (1962), which allows for a minimum at an intermediate growth rate for population, where the factor-price frontier is a tangent to the individual indifference curve.

The empirical findings in the literature concerning the respective elasticities of substitution, our own findings on the r-n relation, and the formal and diagrammatic discussion of the four different cases in the laissez faire framework suggest strongly that there does in fact exist an intermediate optimum growth rate for population in the neoclassical overlapping generations model. In a laissez faire economy, increases in the *growth rate of population only increase steady state utility if the economy is growing on a dynamically inefficient path. The exact sufficient condition for an interior optimum growth rate for population is given by* $\frac{dr}{dn}_{|n=n^*} > 1$*; i.e. in an economy where high (low) growth rates of population lead to a growth path which is efficient (inefficient) there always exists an interior optimum growth rate for population. In all other cases there exists no interior optimum.*

In Chapter 3 we introduced two further aspects into the neoclassical overlapping generations framework: child-dependency costs and government debt. The intention was to examine the robustness of the previous results, which were derived under highly idealized and sterile conditions. The results in Chapters 3 and 4 can be summarized as follows:

1. Arthur and McNicoll (1978) focus on the development of a more precise accounting framework with time as a continuous variable. Children are introduced as a second group of dependents, who independently maximize their expected lifetime utility through borrowing and lending. After all Arthur and McNicoll (1978) claim that by applying their accounting framework to empirical data suggests that the real intergenerational transfer effect turns out to be negative and that population should decline as fast as possible.

   In Chapter 4 the economic dependency ratio was introduced as a criterion, which can be used to calculate actual growth rates that minimize the dependency burden. Contrary to the perspective of Arthur and McNicoll (1978), this alternative approach suggests that there does exist an interior growth rate of population which minimizes the dependency burden despite the fact that children cost resources.

2. Jaeger (1989) reconsiders the validity of the Serendipity Theorem in a three generations model where parents pay and decide on the rearing costs of their children. In this framework, with a fixed-coefficient production function, there are two main conclusions:
   (a) The Serendipity Theorem does not hold in the three generations case as long as children do not voluntarily repay their *exact* rearing costs. There does however, exist a modified Serendipity Theorem, where life-cycle savings are sufficient to support a second-best steady state equilibrium.
   (b) Through an optimal system of social security the government can tax the working age generation and pay benefits to the retired generation, which amount to their exact rearing expenses. This allows to reach the first-best allocation.

In the second part, internal government debt was introduced. Using the framework of Diamond (1965) and De La Croix and Michel (2002), we reconsidered the validity of the Serendipity Theorem and the two-part golden rule under a regime of constant per capita government debt:

1. The social optimum optimorum is not affected by the introduction of government debt. The two-part golden rule still describes the optimal accumulation and consumption patterns in the planned economy.

2. Due to the substitution between debt (paper) and capital in the portfolios of the individuals, the Serendipity Theorem does not

hold anymore. Except for one special case, there does still exist another growth rate for population $\tilde{n}$, which leads the competitive economy to (two-part) golden rule growth.

3. Contrary to the entire previous discussion, this growth rate $\tilde{n}$ is never the optimum growth rate for population. The optimum growth rate leads the competitive economy to an allocation where the marginal productivity of capital exceeds the growth rate of population. The tradeoff, which is relevant on the individual level, is not between wages and interest as in the laissez faire economy discussed in Chapter 2. It is also not between the capital widening effect and the intergenerational transfer effect. Instead, the relevant tradeoff is between the aggregate factor-price effects and the biological interest rate, which the individual receives (after taxes) by holding debt. In such a situation, the relevance of the biological interest rate relations of Samuelson (1958) and Phelps (1961) as the objective ceases.

The Serendipity Theorem holds only under the artificial conditions of the Diamond (1965) model without child-dependency costs, government debt or over-/underfunded social security. In a laissez faire economy with constant per capita debt the growth rate for population, which leads to a golden rule allocation can never be optimal since it balances the wage-interest tradeoff only. The optimum growth rate for population balances the tradeoff between factor-prices and the internal rate of return of the pension scheme. Such an optimum growth rate leads the competitive economy to an allocation where the marginal productivity of capital exceeds the optimum growth rate for population.

A The Bordered Hessian

Substitution of the availability constraint into the utility function leads to a maximization problem with three independent choice variables and a 3x3 Hessian matrix. In this Appendix, we follow the conventional suggestion that the sufficient conditions to a constrained maximization problem should be checked by using the bordered Hessian matrix. We find that the 5x5 bordered Hessian matrix to this maximization problem gives identical necessary and sufficient conditions:

$$\max_{c^1,c^2,k,n,\lambda} \mathcal{L} = U(c^1,c^2) + \lambda(f(k) - (n+\delta)k - c^1 - \frac{c^2}{(1+n)}).$$

The bordered Hessian at the stationary point is given by:

$$\bar{H} = \begin{pmatrix} 0 & -1 & -\frac{1}{(1+n)} & 0 & 0 \\ -1 & U_{c^1c^1} & U_{c^1c^2} & 0 & 0 \\ -\frac{1}{(1+n)} & U_{c^2c^1} & U_{c^2c^2} & 0 & U_{c^1}\frac{1}{(1+n)^2} \\ 0 & 0 & 0 & U_{c^1}f'' & -U_{c^1} \\ 0 & 0 & U_{c^1}\frac{1}{(1+n)^2} & -U_{c^1} & -U_{c^1}\frac{2c^2}{(1+n)^3} \end{pmatrix}.$$

The sufficient conditions for a maximum at c^{1*}, c^{2*}, k^*, n^* and λ^* are (Chiang and Wainwright (2005), p. 362):

$$|\bar{H}_2| > 0; \quad |\bar{H}_3| < 0; \quad |\bar{H}_4| > 0; ......(-1)^n|\bar{H}_n| > 0,$$

for a minimum we have:

$$|\bar{H}_2| < 0; ....|\bar{H}_n| < 0.$$

Using the Laplace expansion we get:

$$\begin{aligned} |\bar{H}_2| &= (-1)|H_1| = \frac{2}{(1+n)}U_{c^1c^2} - \frac{1}{(1+n)^2}U_{c^1c^1} - U_{c^2c^2} > 0, \\ |\bar{H}_3| &= (-1)|H_2| = U_{c^1}f''|\bar{H}_2| < 0, \\ |\bar{H}_4| &= (-1)|H_3| = -|\bar{H}_3|U_{c^1}\frac{2c^2}{(1+n)^3} + U_{c^1}^3 f''\frac{1}{(1+n)^4} - U_{c^1}^2|\bar{H}_2| \lesseqgtr 0. \end{aligned}$$

The relevant three minors lead to the same sufficient conditions for an optimum. Once the choice variable n, which appears only in the constraint is excluded, the sufficient conditions are satisfied: For a given growth rate of population we get the two-part golden rule from the first order conditions, and the sufficient conditions for a local maximum are satisfied.

B Appendix

In our diagrammatic discussion we have shown that the conditions for an interior optimum growth rate of population in the planning framework and the laissez faire framework are the same: For an optimum at n^* it is necessary that the indifference curve in the w, r plane is a tangent to the factor-price frontier (i.e. $\frac{dw}{dr}_{|dU=0} = \phi'(r)$), and it is sufficient that the curvature of the indifference curve is larger than the curvature of the factor-price frontier, i.e. $\frac{d^2w}{dr^2}_{|dU=0} > \phi''(r)$.

We will now proceed by deriving the slope and curvature of the indifference curve and the factor-price frontier. In a second step we will show that the necessary condition for an interior n^* requires that the indifference curve in the w, r plane is a tangent to the factor-price frontier. In a third step we will show that the sufficient condition (86) for a laissez faire optimum at n^*, which was derived from the indirect utility function, is equivalent to $\frac{d^2w}{dr^2}_{|dU=0} > \phi''(r)$. In a last step we show that the conditions for the existence of a laissez faire optimum are identic with those for the planned economy.

Slope and curvature of the indifference curve: The slope of the indifference curve in the w, r space, which is $\frac{-s(w,r)}{(1+r)}$, can be derived as follows:

$$\begin{aligned} U &= U\Big(w - s(w,r), (1+r)s(w,r)\Big) = U(w,r), \\ dU &= U_{c^1}dw - U_{c^1}(s_w dw + s_r dr) + U_{c^2}s(w,r)dr \\ &+ U_{c^2}(s_w dw + s_r dr)(1+r). \end{aligned} \tag{157}$$

With $dU = 0$ and $\frac{U_{c^1}}{U_{c^2}} = (1+r)$ we can rewrite (157) to obtain:

$$\frac{dw}{dr}_{|dU=0} = \frac{-s(w,r)}{(1+r)}. \tag{158}$$

Hence for a constant per capita utility, the real wage is a function $w_{|dU=0} = w(r)$ of the real interest rate. The curvature of this falling indifference curve is:

$$\begin{aligned}\frac{d^2w}{dr^2}_{|dU=0} &= \frac{-(s_w\frac{dw}{dr} + s_r)(1+r) + s(w,r)}{(1+r)^2} \\ &= \frac{s_w s(w,r) - s_r(1+r) + s(w,r)}{(1+r)^2}.\end{aligned} \tag{159}$$

For the following formal discussion it will not be necessary to determine the sign of $\frac{d^2w}{dr^2}_{|dU=0}$. However, at the moment it seems that we cannot rule-out the possibility of concave indifference curves. Hence with respect to the diagrammatic discussion of Case 2 (such an indifference curve is clearly consistent with Case 2, i.e. a minimum at n^*) we cannot rule-out the possibility of an indifference curve, which is concave. With respect to the EIS we have $s_r \geq 0$ for $\sigma \geq 1$ and $s_r < 0$ for $\sigma < 1$, hence a convex indifference curve would be associated with a rather large EIS, which is consistent with the findings of Michel and Pestieau (1993).

Slope and curvature of the factor-price frontier: The factor-price frontier describes the relationship between the marginal products of labor and capital:

$$w = \phi(r); \quad \frac{dw}{dr} = \phi'(r) = -k; \quad \frac{d^2w}{dr^2} = \phi''(r) = \frac{-1}{f''}.$$

This relationship can be obtained along the following line:

$$dw = -kf''dk; \quad dr = f''dk,$$

and hence:

$$\frac{dw}{dr} = -k,$$

with

$$\frac{d(\frac{dw}{dr})}{dk} = -1,$$

and hence:

$$\frac{d^2w}{dr^2} = \frac{-1}{f''}.$$

The elasticity of substitution can thus be related to the curvature of the factor-price frontier:

$$\tau(k) := -\frac{(\frac{r}{w})}{k}\frac{dk}{d(\frac{r}{w})} = -\frac{\frac{r}{w}}{k}(-1)\frac{w^2\phi''}{f(k)} = \frac{rw\phi''}{kf(k)},$$

and hence:

$$\tau = \tau(w, r, \phi'', k); \quad \frac{\partial\tau}{\partial\phi''} > 0,$$

i.e. the larger the elasticity of substitution the larger c.p. the curvature of the factor-price frontier and an interior optimum is less likely.

Compatibility of the diagrammatic and the formal discussion: Using the Serendipity Theorem we can show that the first order condition for a laissez faire/planned optimum at an interior n^* is satisfied if $\phi'(r) = \frac{dw}{dr}_{|dU=0}$ at n^* where:

$$f'(k(n^*)) = n^*; \quad c^{2*} = (1+n^*)s^*,$$

and hence:

$$-k^* + \frac{c^{2*}}{(1+n^*)^2} = 0 \Leftrightarrow -k^* = \frac{-s^*}{\left(1 + f'(k(n^*))\right)}.$$

Q.E.D.

Now we will show that the sufficient condition $\frac{d^2w}{dr^2}_{|dU=0} > \phi''(r)$ can be transformed into condition (86) for a laissez faire optimum at n^*:[82]

$$\frac{s_w s(w,r) - s_r(1+r) + s(w,r)}{(1+r)^2} > \frac{-1}{f''};$$

at the stationary point we have $s = (1+n)k$ and $n = n^* = r$, and hence:

$$\frac{s_w(1+n)k - s_r(1+n) + (1+n)k}{(1+n)} > \frac{-1}{f''}(1+n),$$

this can be rearranged such that:

$$-k < \frac{1}{f''}(1+n) + s_w k - s_r,$$

with $\frac{1}{f''}(1+n) + s_w k - s_r < 0$ by virtue of the stability condition (70). Thus we obtain the sufficient condition (86) for a laissez faire optimum:

$$\frac{-k}{\frac{1}{f''}(1+n) + s_w k - s_r} > 1.$$

Q.E.D.

Compatibility of the conditions for the existence of an interior optimum in the planned and the laissez faire economy: It flows directly from the Serendipity Theorem that the first order conditions for the existence of an interior n^* in the planned economy as well as the laissez faire economy both identify the same stationary point; for $n = n^* = r^*$, conditions (47) and (81) are both satisfied.

We will now show that the same is true for the sufficient conditions. This means that we have to show that the sufficient condition for an optimal interior n^* in the planned economy is only satisfied if $\frac{-k}{\frac{1}{f''}(1+n)+s_w k-s_r} > 1$ at the stationary point.

[82] All endogenous variables are at their optimal values once we set $n = n^*$, but the $*$ is omitted where no misunderstanding is expected.

The second order derivative of the indirect utility function (45) for the planned economy is given by:

$$\frac{d^2U}{dn^2}_{|n=n^*} = U_{c^1}\Big(-\frac{dk_n}{dn} + \frac{(1+n)^2\frac{dc_n^2}{dn} - 2(1+n)c_n^2}{(1+n)^4}\Big) \lesseqqgtr 0. \qquad (160)$$

The sign of this second order derivative hinges on two distinct elements (compare with section 2.3.2.): the first element $\frac{dk_n}{dn}$ is the aspect of optimal capital accumulation. The second element $\frac{(1+n)^2\frac{dc_n^2}{dn} - 2(1+n)c_n^2}{(1+n)^4}$ is concerned with the optimal consumption pattern.

From the first order condition for the optimal capital accumulation pattern we have:

$$r_n = f'(k_n) = n, \quad \frac{dk_n}{dn} = \frac{1}{f''(k_n)}. \qquad (161)$$

For the second element, which is concerned with the optimal consumption pattern, we find that in a planned economy we have:

$$\frac{U_{c^1}(c_n^1, c_n^2)}{U_{c^2}(c_n^1, c_n^2)} = 1 + n,$$

$$w_n = f(k_n) - nk_n - c_n^1 + \frac{c_n^2}{(1+n)^2}.$$

These two equations clearly define an optimal consumption pattern c_n^1 and c_n^2, where $c_n^2 = (1+n)s(w_n, r_n)$; once the individual faces the biological rate of interest it will voluntarily (for all given real wages w_n) choose the optimal (biological) consumption pattern (compare with sections 2.1.3. and 2.1.4.). Hence:

$$\begin{aligned}\frac{dc_n^2}{dn} &= \frac{d[(1+n)s(w_n, r_n)]}{dn} \\ &= s(w_n, r_n) + \Big(s_w\frac{dw_n}{dn} + s_r\frac{dr_n}{dn}\Big)(1+n), \qquad (162)\end{aligned}$$

with:

$$\frac{dr_n}{dn} = 1; \quad \frac{dw_n}{dn} = f'(k_n)\frac{dk_n}{dn} - k_n - n\frac{dk_n}{dn} = -k_n.$$

We can now substitute the expressions in (161) and (162) into (160) to evaluate the sign of $\frac{d^2U}{dn^2}$ at the stationary point, where we have $c_n^{2*} = (1+n^*)s(w^*, r^*) = (1+n^*)^2 k^*$:

$$\begin{aligned} \frac{d^2U}{dn^2}_{|n=n^*} &= U_{c^1}\Big(-\frac{1}{f''(k^*)} + \frac{(1+n^*)^3 k^* + (-s_w k^* + s_r)(1+n^*)^3}{(1+n^*)^4} \\ &- \frac{2(1+n^*)^3 k^*}{(1+n^*)^4}\Big). \end{aligned}$$

Hence $\frac{d^2U}{dn^2}_{|n=n^*}$ is negative if:

$$-k^* < (1+n^*)\frac{1}{f''(k^*)} + s_w k^* - s_r. \tag{163}$$

According to the stability condition (70) we have $(1+n^*)\frac{1}{f''(k^*)} + s_w k^* - s_r < 0$ and we find that at n^* $\frac{d^2U}{dn^2} < 0$ if and only if:

$$\frac{-k^*}{(1+n^*)\frac{1}{f''(k^*)} + s_w k^* - s_r} > 1. \tag{164}$$

This sufficient condition for a social optimum (164) is identical with the sufficient condition (86) for a laissez faire optimum at n^*.

Q.E.D.

C Oscillatory Stability

In this Appendix we will discuss the case of one unique oscillatory steady state equilibrium. The corresponding stability condition is:

$$-1 < \frac{dk_{t+1}}{dk_t} = \frac{-s_w f''k}{(1+n) - s_r f''} < 0; \quad s_w > 0. \tag{165}$$

Since the numerator is positive s_r must be algebraically large and negative, which is only possible for $\sigma < 1$. From the life cycle savings condition (68) we obtain once again:

$$\frac{dk}{dn} = \frac{-k}{s_w f''k + (1+n) - s_r f''}. \tag{166}$$

Utilizing (165) reveals that $\frac{dk}{dn} > 0$ and hence we have $\frac{dr}{dn} < 0$. It is now easy to show that the sufficient condition for an interior optimum growth rate for population is always satisfied:

$$\frac{d^2U}{dn^2}_{|n=n^*} = U_{c^1}\frac{(1-\frac{dr}{dn})}{(1+r)}k\frac{dr}{dn} < 0. \tag{167}$$

Hence we find that an interior minimum is only possible for $0 < \frac{dr}{dn}_{|n=n^*} < 1$, in all other instances we have an interior optimum. However the oscillatory case with $\frac{dk}{dn} > 0$ appears to be rather unrealistic. In addition we note that the claim, that the "stability condition" together with the assumption of normality allows to derive the sign of $\frac{dk}{dn}$, is not quiet accurate. Instead it is necessary to distinguish two cases, in the same manner as in Diamond (1965).

D The crucial r-n relation: Estimates

This Appendix contains three different estimates of the r-n relation:

1. The r-n relation for the United States between 1964 and 1996.
2. The r-n relation for Japan between 1964 and 1998.
3. The average r-n relation for a group of 17 nations between 1963 and 2000.[83] The group consists of:[84] Australia, Austria, Brazil, Canada, Switzerland, Finland, France, Great Britain, India, Italy, Japan, Korea (South), the Netherlands, Norway, New Zealand, Sweden and the United States.

With the United States and Japan we use the world's two largest economies to estimate the response of the net profit rate to the growth rate of the working population. These large countries are the ones where we can expect a rather autonomous movement of the profit rate. The intention with the third regression is to compare the respective average n, r pairs for 17 mostly developed countries. If these 17 countries had a similar tax- and social security-system, a similar savings behavior and a similar "production function", such a comparison might also make some sense, especially since it should capture the long-run implications of differences in the growth rates for population much better than the other regressions which are based on annual changes.

[83] If we included more less developed countries like Brazil and India, we would get better test statistics, and our positive r-n relation would become more significant, if the likes of Mexico, Argentina, Chile, China and Thailand were included. However, we will try not to add apples and oranges in an excessive manner.

[84] The data for Brazil and India is rather incomplete.

Data: The data which is used in the following regressions is taken from the Extended Penn World Tables (V. 2.1). The estimates of the profit rate for the United States in the EPWT appear to be a bit too high if compared to the estimates of Feldstein et al. (1977), (p. 216). However, they seem to be in line with the profit rates which are given in Dumenil et al. (1993), (p. 316).

Method: The discussion between Feldstein et al. (1977)[85] and Dumenil et al. (1993) on the rate of profit reveals that there are severe difficulties associated with estimates that target the movement of the profit rate. In the following we will simply overlook these problems and use the ordinary least squares method – this means we estimate a *linear* r-n relation – to (very) roughly estimate the r-n relation. The only refinement is a time dummy, which accounts for the fact that visual inspection of the data for all 17 countries suggests that the profit rates between 1963 and 1970 are in general higher than those between 1971 and 1998. The scatter plot for the US data (next but one page) with its seven outliers reconfirms this assertion.

Findings: For the United States and Japan we find a highly significant relation between the rate of profit and the growth rate for population. Visual inspection of the respective scatter plots, where each point represents the net profit rate and the growth rate of the working population for the respective year, also suggests that a linear r-n relation is not entirely at odds with the data. We also find that the time dummy is highly significant for both countries. For the United States and Japan we

[85]It might be interesting to note that one can (by visual inspection) find a rate of profit for Japan which is clearly falling (alongside with the growth rate for population).

find in absolute terms 9 and 16 percent higher profit rates for the period between 1964 and 1970.[86] However, due to the severe simplifications, we cannot interpret the rather high R^2 of around $0,8$ as the percentage of variance in the profit rate which is "explained" by the variance in the growth rate of population. The most severe problem is probably that this r-n correlation is more a short-run relation than the steady state impact, which would originate from *permanent* changes in n.

With respect to our main question we can conclude that the first two regressions allow, using the one sided t-test, to refute the null hypothesis $\frac{dr}{dn} < 1$ with a probability of error of less than one percent. The third regression with the sample of 17 countries allows to refute the null hypothesis $\frac{dr}{dn} < 1$ with a probability of error of less than 2,5 percent.

In general we can conclude that these results suggest that real world economies tend to follow a pattern as described by Cases 1 and 4, where (as in Diagram 8) the rate of profit increases faster than the growth rate for population (this claim implies that we believe that the current growth rates for population are larger than n^*, or alternatively, that the r-n relation is actually almost linear). Another point is that the scatter plot for the 17 countries suggests that the net profit rates for all countries tend to be much larger than the growth rates of population (this should hold even if we added exogenous technical progress and allowed for some modest time discount factor). However, according to condition (146) this does not mean that the current growth rates for population are not optimal. Another point (we do not give the graphs) is that even for very

[86]Dumenil et al. (1993), (p. 316) find a similar large increase totaling 16 percent in the US profit rate during and after World War II.

small countries like Switzerland one can find that the rate of profit and the rate of growth of the working population are closely related.

Dependent Variable: net profit rate USA
Method: Least Squares
Date: 10/18/06 Time: 12:27
Sample (adjusted): 1964 1996
Included observations: 33 after adjustments

Variable	Coefficient	Std. Error	t-Statistic	Prob.
C	0.132169	0.012962	10.19691	0.0000
n	3.856228	0.730278	5.280492	0.0000
DUMMY '64-'70	0.090096	0.008659	10.40460	0.0000

R-squared	0.814067	Mean dependent var	0.215964
Adjusted R-squared	0.801672	S.D. dependent var	0.045614
S.E. of regression	0.020314	Akaike info criterion	-4.868511
Sum squared resid	0.012380	Schwarz criterion	-4.732464
Log likelihood	83.33042	F-statistic	65.67428
Durbin-Watson stat	1.116879	Prob(F-statistic)	0.000000

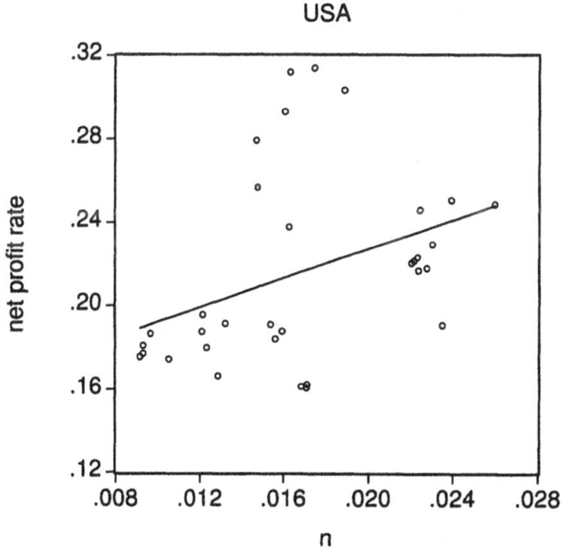

Dependent Variable: net profit rate Japan
Method: Least Squares
Date: 10/18/06 Time: 12:37
Sample (adjusted): 1964 1998
Included observations: 35 after adjustments

Variable	Coefficient	Std. Error	t-Statistic	Prob.
C	0.078265	0.012627	6.198251	0.0000
n	4.808601	1.511270	3.181827	0.0032
DUMMY '64-'70	0.157705	0.021689	7.271098	0.0000

R-squared	0.867543	Mean dependent var	0.154186
Adjusted R-squared	0.859265	S.D. dependent var	0.093037
S.E. of regression	0.034903	Akaike info criterion	-3.790691
Sum squared resid	0.038982	Schwarz criterion	-3.657376
Log likelihood	69.33710	F-statistic	104.7940
Durbin-Watson stat	1.172615	Prob(F-statistic)	0.000000

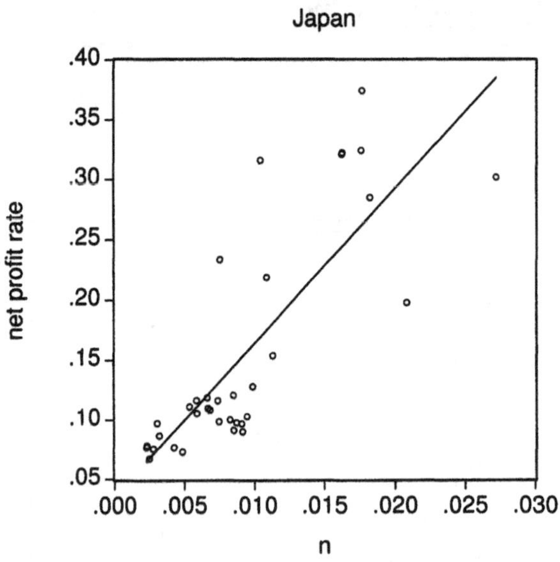

Dependent Variable: average net profit rate 1963-2000				
Method: Least Squares				
Date: 10/23/06 Time: 16:03				
Sample (adjusted): 1 17				
Included observations: 17 after adjustments				
Variable	Coefficient	Std. Error	t-Statistic	Prob.
C	0.101335	0.032935	3.076813	0.0077
average n 1963-2000	6.281249	2.236013	2.809130	0.0132

R-squared	0.344727	Mean dependent var	0.183414
Adjusted R-squared	0.301042	S.D. dependent var	0.074952
S.E. of regression	0.062663	Akaike info criterion	-2.591969
Sum squared resid	0.058899	Schwarz criterion	-2.493944
Log likelihood	24.03174	F-statistic	7.891209
Durbin-Watson stat	1.914507	Prob(F-statistic)	0.013214

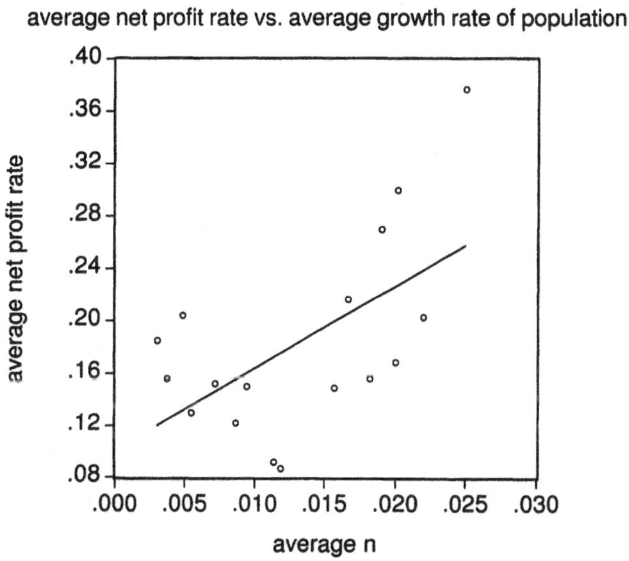

E Appendix

After having completed the entire work on this thesis, the author made the discovery that a r, n and w, r diagram similar to Diagram 12 for the Cases 1 and 2 can be found in Phelps (1968), (pp. 504-505). However, Phelps (1968) does not provide a consequent formal treatment. Furthermore we can find "our" Theorem 2 in Phelps (1968). This means that our unbiased intention to summarize and supplement the key points of the Deardorff-Samuelson 1975 – 1976 exchange led to a diagrammatic representation, which was to a certain extend and in a different context already given in 1968 by Phelps. In addition one can find that Phelps (1968), (pp. 517-518) shows that a competitive Cobb-Douglas framework is consistent with Case 2 i.e. an interior minimum at n^*. Thus, in the light of the Serendipity Theorem, it should have been no surprise to Samuelson (1975a), Deardorff (1976) and Samuelson (1976) to find that there is an interior minimum in the Cobb-Douglas case.

However, the Phelps (1968) essay is vague (Isbister (1969) accuses Phelps of "occasional error") and does not give a rigorous treatment of the problem. The decisive points are relegated to the Appendix (II) and Phelps (1968) does not make a clear commitment to his reasoning. Another point is that Phelps, who also considers the pleasures of parenthood, states: "... it cannot be assumed that $\bar{n}$ is in any sense the "optimum" ..." (Phelps (1968), p. 505), where $\bar{n}$ is the optimal n^* of Samuelson (1975a).

After all it appears that some of the elements to the problem of optimal population can be found directly in Diamond (1965) (Diamond (1965) actually solves for n^* in the Cobb-Douglas case). Phelps (1968) makes some more of these elements visible (without the clear intention to focus on one particular subject (see the Phelps (1969), (pp. 460-461) reply to Isbister (1969)). The clear intention to derive an n^* in an economy without the pleasures of parenthood and a consequent treatment, as the entire literature on the matter suggests, [87] can be found in the Samuelson-Deardorff exchange. It is also bewildering that Phelps never commented on the Samuelson (1975a), Samuelson (1975b), Deardorff (1976) and Samuelson (1976) essays.

[87]Arthur and McNicoll (1978) are the only ones who refer to the Phelps (1968) essay, however, they refer to the Deardorff (1976) essay when it comes to the sufficient conditions and the Cobb-Douglas case.

F Pay-as-you-go Social Security and optimal population

In this Appendix we will briefly substantiate the claim that the qualitative conditions for an interior optimum in an economy with debt are similar to those for an economy with a pay-as-you-go social security system. Once we denote the per capita contributions by α and the old age benefits by β, the budget constraint for the social security can be written as:

$$N_t\alpha = N_{t-1}\beta \quad \Leftrightarrow \quad (1+n)\alpha = \beta. \tag{168}$$

Hence the representative individual living in a steady state equilibrium is affected by demographic change according to:

$$U(n) = U(w(k) - \alpha - (1+n)k, \beta + (1+n)(1+f'(k))k).$$

Utilizing (168) and the respective factor prices gives:

$$U(n) = U(f(k) - f'k - \alpha - (1+n)k, (1+n)\alpha + (1+n)(1+f')k).$$

Hence the first order condition, after some cancelling of terms, for the optimum growth rate is given by:

$$\frac{dU}{dn} = U_{c^1}\frac{\alpha}{(1+f')} + U_{c^1}\frac{(n-f')k}{(1+f')}\frac{dr}{dn} = 0. \tag{169}$$

Comparison between (169) and (146) reveals that once again, the tradeoff is between the increased internal rate of return of the pension system $U_{c^1}\frac{\alpha}{(1+f')}$ and the two factor prices $U_{c^1}\frac{(n-f')k}{(1+f')}\frac{dr}{dn}$.

The key difference between the constant per capita debt policy and the pay-as-you go social security system is that the contribution rate α does not enter the second term. The reason for this is the following:

In an economy with pay-as-you-go pension scheme, the (constant) contribution rate to the system is independent from the growth rate for population. In the economy with government debt there is a link between the amount of resources, which are distributed by the government and the growth rate for population: The tax on the young generation is given by $\tau^1(k) = (f'(k(n)) - n)b)$. Hence, once the growth rate for population is changed the tax rate also changes and thus the total amount of resources which goes through the hands of the government, which yield the biological rate of return.

G Formal aspects to Diagram 16

Individual utility is given by:

$$U = U\Big(w(n) - s(\tilde{w}(n), r(n)) - (r(n) - n)b, (1 + r(n))s(\tilde{w}(n), r(n))\Big),$$

by varying the growth rate for population only, we obtain the following slope for the indifference curve:

$$\frac{dw}{dr}_{|dU=0, \frac{U_{c1}}{U_{c2}}=1+r, dn\neq 0} = b - \frac{s}{1+r} - \frac{dn}{dr}b.$$

We can now reproduce the first order condition (146) by setting $\frac{dw}{dr}_{|dU=0, \frac{U_{c1}}{U_{c2}}=(1+r)} = \phi'(r) = -k$:

$$b - \frac{s}{(1+r)} - \frac{dn}{dr}b = -k \quad \Leftrightarrow \quad \frac{n-r}{1+r}(k+b)\frac{dr}{dn} + b = 0.$$

For $n = \tilde{n} = r$ we have:

$$\frac{dw}{dr} = b - \frac{s}{(1+r)} - b\frac{dn}{dr} < -k,$$

since,

$$-b\frac{dn}{dr} < 0.$$

Hence at $\tilde{n}$ the slope of the indifference curve is algebraically larger than that of the factor-price frontier.

References

Allais, M. (1947). Economie et interet. *Imprimerie Nationale.*

Arrow, K. J., Chenery, H., Minhas, B. S., and Solow, R. M. (1961). Capital-labor substitution and economic efficiency. *Review of Economics and Statistics*, (Vol. 43):225–250.

Arthur, W. B. and McNicoll, G. (1977). Optimal time paths with age-dependency: A theory of population policy. *The Review of Economic Studies*, (Vol. 44, No. 1):111–123.

Arthur, W. B. and McNicoll, G. (1978). Samuelson, population and intergenerational transfers. *International Economic Review*, (Vol. 19, No. 1):241–246.

Barro, R. and Sala-I-Martin, X. (1995). *Economic Growth.* New York [u.a.]: McGraw-Hill, internat. edition.

Blanchard, O. J. and Fischer, S. (1989). *Lectures on Macroeconomics.* Cambridge, Mass. [u.a.]: MIT Press.

Bommier, A. and Lee, R. D. (2003). Overlapping generations models with realistic demography. *Journal of Population Economics*, (Vol. 16):135–160.

Börsch-Supan, A., Ludwig, A., and Winter, J. (2006). Aging, pension reform, and capital flows: A multi-country simulation model. *Economica*, (73):625–658.

Cass, D., Okuno, M., and Zilcha, I. (1979). The role of money in supporting the pareto optimality of competitive equilibrium in consumption-loan type models. *Journal of Economic Theory*, (20):41–80.

Cass, D. and Yaari, M. E. (1966). A re-examination of the pure consumption loans model. *The Journal of Political Economy*, (Vol. 74, No. 4):353–367.

Cass, D. and Yaari, M. E. (1967). Individual saving, aggregate capital accumulation, and efficient growth. In *Essays on the Theory of Optimal Economic Growth*, pages 233–268. ed. Karl Shell, MIT Press.

Chiang, A. C. (1992). *Elements of Dynamic Optimization*. McGraw-Hill, Inc.

Chiang, A. C. and Wainwright, K. (2005). *Fundamental Methods of Mathematical Economics*. Boston [u.a.]: McGraw-Hill, 4. internat. edition.

de Abreu Pessoa, S., Pessoa, S. M., and Rob, R. (2005). Elasticity of substitution between capital and labor and its applications to growth and development. *PIER Working Paper*, (05-012):1–50.

De La Croix, D. and Michel, P. (2002). *A Theory of Economic Growth*. Cambridge: Cambridge Univ. Press.

Deardorff, A. V. (1976). The optimum growth rate for population: Comment. *International Economic Review*, (Vol. 17, No. 2 (Jun., 1976)):510–515.

Diamond, P. A. (1965). National debt in a neoclassical growth model. *The American Economic Review*, (Vol. 55, No. 5, Part 1 (Dec., 1965)):1126–1150.

Drucker, P. (1997). The future that has already happened. *Harvard Business Review*, (Vol. 75, No.5):20–24.

Dumenil, G., Glick, M., and Levy, D. (1993). The rise of the rate of profit during world war II. *The Review of Economics and Statistics*, (Vol. 75, No. 2.):315–320.

Feess, E. (1997). *Mikroökonomie.* Metropolis.

Feldstein, M. (1974). Social security, induced retirement, and aggregate capital accumulation. *The Journal of Political Economy*, (Vol. 82, No. 5):905–926.

Feldstein, M., Summers, L., and Wachter, M. (1977). Is the rate of profit falling? *Brookings Papers on Economic Activity*, (Vol. 1977, No. 1.):211–228.

Friedman, M. (1999). Speaking the truth about social security reform. *Cato Institute Briefing Papers*, (No. 46):1–3.

Gravelle, H. and Rees, R. (1992). *Microeconomics.* London [u.a.]: Longman, 2. edition.

Guvenen, M. F. (2002). Reconciling conflicting evidence on the elasticity of intertemporal substitution: A macroeconomic perspective. *Working Paper: Rochester Center for Economic Research*, (No. 491):1–37.

Harrod, R. F. (1939). An essay in dynamic theory. *Economic Journal*, (Vol. 49):14–33.

Homburg, S. (1987). *Theorie der Alterssicherung.* Springer Verlag.

Isbister, J. (1969). Population increase: A comment. *The Canadian Journal of Economics*, (Vol. 2, No.3):455–459.

Jaeger, K. (1972). *Altersstruckturveränderungen der Bevölkerung Ersparnis und wirtschaftliches Wachstum.* Duncker und Humblot Berlin.

Jaeger, K. (1980). *Wachstumstheorie.* Kohlhammer Verlag.

Jaeger, K. (1981). Ökonomisches Gleichgewicht. *HdWW*, (Bd. 3):671–699.

Jaeger, K. (1989). The serendipity theorem reconsidered: The three-generations case without inheritance. In *Economic theory of optimal population*, pages 75–87. ed. Klaus F. Zimmermann, Springer.

Jaeger, K. (2002). Kinder, Rentner und die "optimale" Wachstumsrate der Bevölkerung. *Jahrbuch für Wirtschaftswissenschaften*, (Vol. 53, No. 3):269–289.

Jaeger, K. and Kuhle, W. (2007). The optimum growth rate for population reconsidered. *MEA Discussion Paper*, (147-2007):1–20.

Jones, H. G. (1975). *An Introduction to Modern Theories of Economic Growth.* London: Nelson.

Keynes, J. M. (1978). Some economic consequences of a declining population. *Population and Development Review*, (Vol. 4, No. 3.):517–523.

Krüger, D. and Ludwig, A. (2007). On the consequences of demographic change for rates of return to capital, and the distribution of wealth and welfare. *Journal of Monetary Economics*, (54):49–87.

Lerner, A. P. (1959). Consumption-loan interest and money. *The Journal of Political Economy*, (Vol. 67, No. 5):512–518.

Malthus, T. R. (1992). *An Essay on the Principle of Population.* Cambridge: Cambridge Univ. Press.

Meade, J. E. (1937). *Economic Analysis and Policy.* Oxford University Press, 2. edition.

Michel and Pestieau (1993). Population growth and optimality: When does serendipity hold. *Journal of Population Economics*, (Vol. 6, No. 4):353–362.

Nerlove, M., Razin, A., and Sadka, E. (1986). Some welfare implications of endogenous fertility. *International Economic Review*, (Vol. 27, No.1):3–31.

Ogaki, M. and Reinhart, C. M. (1998). Measuring intertemporal substitution: The role of durable goods. *Journal of Political Economy*, (Vol. 106, No.5):1078–1098.

Persson and Tabellini (2000). *Political Economics.* MIT Press.

Phelps, E. (1961). The golden rule of accumulation: A fable for growthmen. *The American Economic Review*, (Vol. 51, No. 4):638–643.

Phelps, E. (1967a). The golden rule of procreation. In *Golden Rules of Economic Growth*, pages 176–183. ed. Edmund Phelps, North Holland Publishing Company, Amsterdam.

Phelps, E. (1967b). The meaning and existence of the golden rule path. In *Golden Rules of Economic Growth*, pages 3–20. ed. Edmund Phelps, North Holland Publishing Company, Amsterdam.

Phelps, E. (1968). Population increase. *The Canadian Journal of Economics*, (Vol. 1, No.3):497–518.

Phelps, E. (1969). Population increase: Reply. *The Canadian Journal of Economics*, (Vol. 2, No.3):459–461.

Rodriguez, A. (1988). The dependency ratio and optimum population growth. The total utility case. *Journal of Population Economics*, (Vol. 1):141–156.

Samuelson, P. A. (1941). The stability of equilibrium: Comparative statics and dynamics. *Econometrica*, (Vol. 9, No. 2.):97–120.

Samuelson, P. A. (1958). An exact consumption-loan model of interest with or without the social contrivance of money. *The Journal of Political Economy*, (Vol. 66, No. 6):467–482.

Samuelson, P. A. (1959). Consumption-loan interest and money: Reply. *The Journal of Political Economy*, (Vol. 67, No. 5):518–522.

Samuelson, P. A. (1961). *Foundations of Economic Analysis*. Harvard University Press.

Samuelson, P. A. (1962). Parable and realism in capital theory: The surrogate production function. *Reviev of Economic Studies*, (29):193–206.

Samuelson, P. A. (1966). A summing-up. *The Quarterly Journal of Economics*, pages 568–83.

Samuelson, P. A. (1968). The two-part golden rule deduced as the asymptotic turnpike of catenary motions. *Western Economic Journal*, (VI , March, 1968):85–89.

Samuelson, P. A. (1975a). The optimum growth rate for population. *International Economic Review*, (Vol. 16, No. 3):531–538.

Samuelson, P. A. (1975b). Optimum social security in a life-cycle growth model. *International Economic Review*, (Vol. 16, No. 3):539–544.

Samuelson, P. A. (1976). The optimum growth rate for population: Agreement and evaluations. *International Economic Review*, (Vol. 17, No. 2):516–525.

Schmitt-Rink, G. (1989). Is there an optimal growth rate for population? In *Economic theory of optimal population*, pages 51–63. ed. Klaus F. Zimmermann, Springer.

Solow, R. M. (1956). A contribution to the theory of economic growth. *The Quarterly Journal of Economics*, (Vol. 70, No. 1):65–94.

Weil, D. N. (1999). Population growth, dependency, and consumption. *The American Economic Review*, (Vol. 89, No.2):251–255.

Wilkinson, L. P. (1978). Classical approaches to population and family planning. *Population and Development Review*, (Vol. 4, No. 3.):439–455.

Ludger J. Löning

Economic Growth, Biodiversity Conservation, and the Formation of Human Capital in a Developing Country

The Case of Guatemala

Frankfurt am Main, Berlin, Bern, Bruxelles, New York, Oxford, Wien, 2004.
XVIII, 246 pp., 19 fig., 38 tab.
Göttingen Studies in Development Economics. Edited by Hermann Sautter.
Vol. 13
ISBN 978-3-631-52607-1 · pb. € 45.50*

Can education play a role in fostering economic growth and simultaneously decrease pressure on forests? The aim of this study is to show that it can. Human capital formation is a key element in a development strategy that includes natural resource conservation within the framework of sustained economic growth and poverty alleviation. Consequently, it is not by chance that Guatemala is experiencing both minimal per capital income growth and high deforestation while having one of the lowest educational levels in Latin America. However, since many assumptions about educational benefits are controversial and many aspects depend on broader issues, human capital formation can only be one piece in a multidimensional puzzle. This study is organized into three parts, each one of which can be read independently: first, a macroeconomic assessment of education and other factors involved in the country's growth trajectory; second, a rural analysis indicating the root causes of deforestation and the role education can play to slow down habitat loss; third, the highlighting of some elements indispensable to reform and to subsequent improvement of the quality of rural schooling.

Contents: Patterns of Growth in Guatemala · Measuring the Contribution of Education to Growth · Data Compilation in a Post-Conflict Country · Empirical Evidence for Guatemala · and many more

Kolibri 360 GmbH
Ferdinand-Jühlke-Straße 7
99095 Erfurt, Deutschland
produktsicherheit@kolibri360.de

Druck:
CPI Druckdienstleistungen GmbH
im Auftrag der
Kolibri 360 GmbH
Ferdinand-Jühlke-Str. 7
99095 Erfurt